THE LIVING PAST

The Living Past

CYRUS H. GORDON

illustrated

THE JOHN DAY COMPANY, NEW YORK

Designed by Robert Josephy

PRINTED IN THE UNITED STATES OF AMERICA

Van Rees Press · New York

These pages are affectionately dedicated

to my mother

who taught me that anything worth doing

is worth doing well

and to my father

who instilled in me a love of learning

PREFACE

FOR some time I have been seeking to render my parents some of the obedience I failed to show them when I was a child. Several months ago my resolve to be a good son was put to a severe test when my father addressed me thus: "For quite a few years you have been publishing learned monographs and articles that may possibly be all right but that neither your family nor friends can understand. I want you to write a popular book so that plain human beings with merely one or two college degrees may know what you are talking about." Now ten years before this, a notorious popularizer of Biblical archaeology had asked me what I thought of a theory he was about to publish in a Sunday School paper. Since the theory was contrary to the facts I told him why I disagreed. "Scientifically you are right," he retorted, "but I shall publish it just the same. After all, it's only for the public." Subsequent experience has intensified my distaste for popularizing as it is generally done. But inasmuch as I had decided to abide by my father's wish, I set myself to devising a plan for writing a popular book without relinquishing standards of accuracy. I therefore determined to limit myself to material that I control

7

critically from the sources even though this often means sacrificing breadth for depth and quantity for quality.

The subject of this book is a sort of cross section of a decade of exploration, excavation, and armchair research. In spite of a seeming disparity among the archaeological, artistic, and inscriptional material, there is a higher unity born of the oneness of purpose that led me to all of these topics. Each subject is, so to speak, a figure on the single, great unfinished canvas on which I am trying to delineate life throughout the ages in the Near East. That the gaps are more extensive than the figures is only to be expected. I estimate that I shall have to work on my "canvas" for thirty or forty more years before I can complete it.

I do not treat all the material in the same way. In the archaeological chapters, I stress method; in the others, content. I have done so because laymen tend to be more interested in how the archaeologist works and lives than in the walls and potsherds he finds. But since reading is a familiar process, it is not so necessary to dwell on the methods of epigraphy, linguistics, and philology that enable the scholar to interpret texts correctly. The artistic material I treat as human documents—not as art for art's sake; my approach is that of the historian, not of the art critic. If the aesthete is offended by this attitude, I would remind him that until the art historian dates, describes, and interprets a class of art objects, the art critic is often quite unable to deal with it.

I hope the serious reader will not look askance at some of the personal reminiscences included in the archaeological sections. My field work brought me into contact with the Arab world from 1931 to 1935, and I found that a knowledge of present-day life in the Near East is just as valuable for understanding the history of those lands as a knowledge of the history is for comprehending the present-day life. If my studies have taught me anything it is that the human race is one in time and, for that matter, in place. I am a humanist, and antiquity interests me not because it is old but because it is human. In any case, my anecdotes (even the flippant ones) of living Arabs are humanistic source material, and the foregoing sentences constitute an explanation rather than an apology.

In order to reduce my professional pedantry to a minimum, I first delivered the following chapters as a series of informal talks to such students and faculty of Smith College as cared to listen. President Herbert Davis enabled me to secure the assistance of my colleague Miss Ruth Agnew, who took down those talks stenographically. Her typed transcript was the rough draft of this book. I am deeply indebted to Mr. Davis for his co-operation and to Miss Agnew for her skillful assistance. I am also grateful to my friends Doctors Wm. F. Albright, H. Louis Ginsberg, Nelson Glueck, Edith Porada, Pierre Purves, and Ovid Sellers to whom I parceled out the chapters in manuscript for their valuable criticism. It is a pleasure to thank Professor Millar Burrows, president of the American Schools of Oriental Research, for permission to use photographs taken at sites excavated by the Schools.

I would call the attention of my fellow orientalists to the fact that this book is of scientific value, if for no other reason, because of the hitherto unpublished monuments in the plates. It is such source material that has a lasting value, outliving the words that are written about it. But I should like to remark that in restudying the sources in preparation for this popular account I have learned things of scholarly worth that I should otherwise have missed. For example, in rereading the Ugaritic poems with a view to telling their story to the layman, I discovered things I had failed to observe when I studied those texts for composing my *Ugaritic Grammar*.

To the layman I would address a few words of caution. I have not rehashed old stuff for you. Most of my material is newly unearthed, recently published or even hitherto unpublished. I have taken every reasonable measure to omit questionable data or at least to indicate where doubt exists. But with all my good intentions, some mistakes have doubtless remained. Would that I could say with Mohammed: "There is no error in this book." But as it is, I plead in the words of the Psalmist: "Errors, who can perceive them? Acquit me of hidden [transgressions]!"

CONTENTS

Introduction   15

I   Exploring Edom and Moab   21

II   A Minor Expedition among the
      "Lions" of Ader   42

III   Sites of Simple Stratification   51

IV   Mounds of Many Cities   60

V   Graves and Other "Intrusions"   92

VI   Glyptic Art   113

VII   The Gods and Heroes of Ugarit   133

VIII Private and Public Life in Nuzu   156

IX   Military Correspondence from
      the Last Days of Judah   179

X   A World of Demons and Liliths   196

XI   The Past Still Lives   218

      Bibliographical Suggestions   221

      Index   225

ILLUSTRATIONS

FACING PAGE

The Temple of Bacchus at Baalbek: an unusually fine example of the Hellenistic architecture that the Nabateans adapted to the carving of cities like Petra out of mountain walls.   64

The mound of Tepe Gawra, as viewed from the northwest, after the removal of the eight upper levels.   65

At work on Tepe Gawra: removing Level VIII so as to reach the earlier town below it.   80

Unearthing the buried cities at Tell Beit Mirsim.   80

The Iraqi machine-gun squad that kept the peace in Bashiqa during Ramadan.   81

A Yezidi, the author, and an oriental Christian, in the mountains of Kurdistan.   81

Mr. William Gad, surveying the walls at Level A at Tell Beit Mirsim, assisted by two local boys.   112

An infant burial at Tepe Gawra.   113

A double burial at Tepe Gawra. A hand of the skeleton on the left is in its mouth.   113

Reproductions of thirty-two ancient cylinder seals.   118-132

13

FACING PAGE

The farming implements of the Arab peasant today are far less developed than the plowing-and-sowing machine of Cassite Babylonia (see seal 28 in Chapter VI). Here is a Syrian farmer tilling the soil with a primitive plow drawn by a humped ox.   142

Syrian boys on their donkeys. Little donkeys such as those on which the goddess Asherah and the hero Daniel rode are still quite common in the Near East.   143

The Aramaic incantation in cuneiform from Uruk—Obverse   198

The Aramaic incantation in cuneiform from Uruk—Reverse   199

This photograph of an Aramaic bowl was made with a special lens so that the incantation on the concave surface appears without distortion.   202

An aerial view of Nuzu. Such a photograph is an important archaeological aid, providing an excellent record of the completed excavation.   203

MAPS

The Near East   20

Southern Palestine and Transjordan   24

Assyria   63

INTRODUCTION

ONE might imagine that the battles raging in the Near and Middle East would bring home the fundamental lesson that since mankind is one, isolation is unrealistic. But, while the impact of events has at last brought most of us to the realization that at least the Anglo-Saxon democracies are living in the same world, the great majority of our fellow citizens are still far from recognizing that the entire world is a unit and that the wars in Africa and Asia will have serious consequences for us. We would be substantially better off if only all our statesmen would rise above a narrow view of geography. But it is even harder to overcome intellectual than political isolationism, for intellectual maturity demands a sense of an evolving unity throughout time as well as a broad conception of geography.

The bearing of the ancient Near East on the modern Occident happens to be striking as well as fundamental, and a few random illustrations ought to bring this out sufficiently for present purposes:

1. All practicing Christians worship Yahweh, Who started out as the god of one or more Canaanite tribes.

2. The Ten Commandments and the teachings of the

Hebrew prophets (in both Testaments) are the foundation of Western morality, ethics, and much of the law.

3. Our most English-sounding names, like John and Mary or David and Susan, are good Hebrew.

4. The Sabbath, perhaps the most important labor legislation next to the abolition of slavery, is a Hebrew institution.

5. The witches of New England were done to death in fulfillment of a Hebrew law.

6. Our Mormons justified polygamy because it conformed with the Semitic patriarchal system in Scripture.

7. The words of Jesus, now become articles of faith in the Occident, were spoken in Aramaic to the Jews of Palestine.

8. We use the Phoenician alphabet that reached us through Greek and Roman channels.

9. Easter baffles us so with its wanderings around our solar calendar because our celebration of that holiday still hinges on the lunar calendar of the ancient Babylonians.

10. We call some of the planets by their Babylonian names; for example, Venus is simply the Latin equivalent of Ishtar.

11. We follow the sexagesimal system of the Sumerians in more ways than one, of which the most remarkable is perhaps the division of the circle into 360 degrees.

A significant difference between our oriental and classical heritages is that the evidence for the former is in the process of emerging from the soil, whereas our knowledge of the latter has been more or less fixed for a long time. Our Near East heritage is so basic that new discoveries often throw back the origins of our culture by centuries and even millennia. To take an example that brings into play both Hebrew and non-Hebraic records: Shakespeare, in making Shylock say: "A Daniel come to judgment," refers to the Daniel of the apocryphal History of Susanna (not the canonical Book of Daniel). This Daniel is a Canaanite hero of justice, and the sources of his motif have recently been thrown back to the fourteenth century B.C. by the excavations at Ugarit (See Chapter VII) which yielded a whole epic about this Daniel of justice. In rereading Milton, Shakespeare, or countless other authors, any scholar who keeps abreast of the rich discoveries in the Near East could make many such fresh contributions to the "sources behind the sources" of English literature. For the Bible has always exercised a direct and potent influence on English-speaking people, and the Near East happens to be the world in which the Bible evolved. I should like to say much more about Near East influence upon us, through non-Hebraic as well as Biblical channels, but this is not the place to do so.

Near East archaeology has been making far richer contributions to our knowledge of human history than any other branch of investigation. A century ago one could not speak of history, in any strict sense of the word, before the time of Abraham (around 1900 B.C.) —with the partial exception of the tenth chapter of Genesis. Indeed much of the history after his time had come down to us in a sketchy or not-too-authentic way. Now, however, we have a controlled history that goes well beyond 3000 B.C. with written records in Mesopotamia and Egypt. We have also the rich archaeological remains from stratified cities spanning the fifth, and perhaps stretching back into the sixth, millennium B.C. Near East archaeology has thus greatly widened our knowledge of men who built cities. Much more is left to be done than has been done; for every mound excavated in the Near East, a hundred remain untouched. Besides, most of the excavated mounds have been dug only in small part.

In the following pages we shall see how the explorer discovers mounds in Western Asia and how the excavator digs them; what the finds are and what they reveal. The results of such investigations are the legacy of members of the human race to which we all belong. I hope the reader will not regard the contents of this book as an escape from the present world but rather as a key to part of it.

THE LIVING PAST

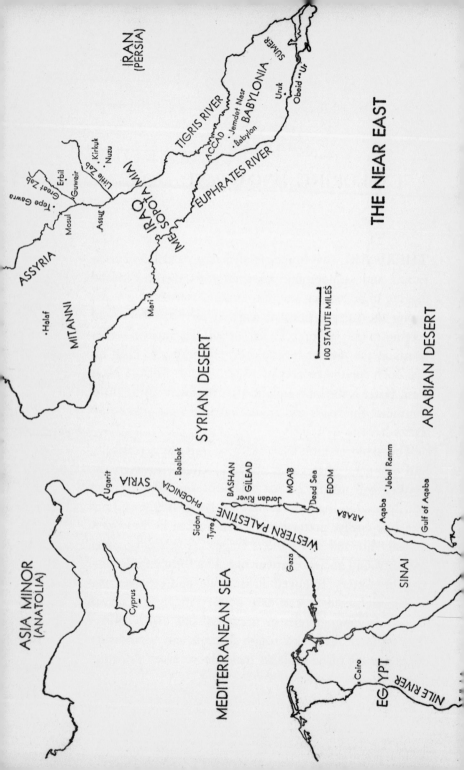

THE NEAR EAST

IRAN
(PERSIA)

ASSYRIA

MITANNI

•Halaf

•Tepe Gawra
Great Zab
Erbil
•Guweir
Mosul
Little Zab
Kirkuk
Nuzu
•Assur

IRAQ

MESOPOTAMIA

TIGRIS RIVER

ACCAD
•Jemdet Nasr
•Babylon

BABYLONIA

SUMER

Uruk
Obeid •••Ur

EUPHRATES RIVER

•Mari

SYRIAN DESERT

100 STATUTE MILES

ARABIAN DESERT

ASIA MINOR
(ANATOLIA)

Cyprus

Ugarit
SYRIA
•Baalbek
PHOENICIA

BASHAN
GILEAD
Jordan River
MOAB
Dead Sea
EDOM
ARABA
Aqaba •Jebel Ramm
Gulf of Aqaba

Sidon
Tyre
WESTERN PALESTINE
Gaza

MEDITERRANEAN SEA

SINAI

•Cairo

EGYPT
NILE RIVER

CHAPTER I

EXPLORING EDOM AND MOAB

THERE ARE two branches of field archaeology: excavation and exploration. Excavation is the methodical digging of an ancient site. Exploration consists of investigating the surface finds of a given territory. First and foremost, the explorer looks for all the ancient settlements in the district he explores. He must also keep his eye open for the sources of water, because, in the Near East, water is the most sought-after necessity of life. Furthermore, the roads and trade routes and national boundaries have to be traced.

The explorer goes over the given area systematically and examines whatever is above ground. However, the pottery will usually be his chief criterion. Pottery was widely used in the historic periods. Being fragile and not as a rule costly, pottery was often broken in the course of daily life and so countless fragments generally cover and surround ancient settlements. The form and decoration of pottery followed fickle style and so the competent archaeologist can date pottery much as some of us can date automobiles or dresses of our own century. The explorer also makes rough sketches and occasionally takes out his plane table to make more exact drawings of architectural monuments that have survived above ground. He locates each place on his map and does everything that can reasonably be done to describe the ancient site by a cursory examination.

Transjordan, or Palestine east of the Jordan Rift, is not sufficiently known and has therefore been in need of archaeological study. In antiquity it was divided into the following countries from north to south: Bashan, famed for its rich men and their pampered wives; Gilead, whose balm has become proverbial; Ammon, occupying the central position; Moab, the land of Ruth; and Edom, which perhaps stretched on both sides of the Rift. All of these nations in antiquity belonged to a group of people called the Canaanites. Culturally and linguistically they were practically identical with the Judean and Israelite "Canaanites" west of the Rift. Indeed some of the Israelite tribes lived in Transjordan. It was Yahwism that distinguished the two Hebrew nations from the other Canaanites and it was the great Hebrew prophets who transformed their little "Canaanite" people into one of the great factors of world history.

Transjordan today is a very different land from Western Palestine. The latter, with its holy sites, has been attracting many visitors from distant lands, especially since the Crusades, and has therefore become largely occidentalized. Transjordan, however, is still an unspoiled Arab country, where men are, according to our standards, quite wild, and where occidental civilization has not made any serious encroachments. Tribes wander there, subject to the law of the desert, and men armed with loaded rifles walk and ride the length and breadth of the land.

It was in the spring of 1934 that it was decided to launch our expedition from Jerusalem. We had a Chevrolet truck in which we packed our supplies. The importance of ceramics to the explorer was reflected in the numerous bags we took along so as to keep the pottery finds from being mixed up. We had to have at least one bag for every site we might possibly examine. In addition to that, we had our photographic equipment; for in archaeological work it is not too much of an exaggeration to say there is no such thing as too many pictures. We had a diary for recording a detailed account of our discoveries, and drawing equipment for making plans. Each man had a sleeping bag; for like the Arabs, we were to be the guests of Allah, with no roof over our head but God's heaven. The sleeping bag is large enough to hold a fairly tall man; blankets are inside, and at night you crawl in and make yourself as comfortable as you can. Mother earth does not make a comfortable couch during the first couple of nights out, but thereafter one almost forgets about beds. We brought very little foodstuff and cooking equipment because we planned to live off the land as much as we could. For each man, we took a canteen to hold the most precious of all supplies—water. Nor did we forget mosquito netting, quinine, and a first-aid kit.

The director, Dr. Nelson Glueck, and I were the only ones to start from Jerusalem. We drove eastward, down and down the winding road, until an hour later we had

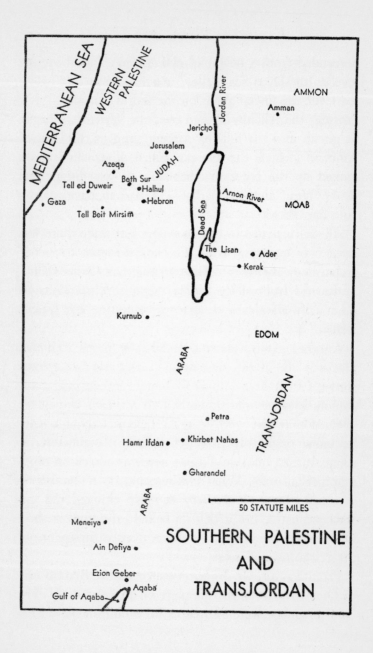

MEDITERRANEAN SEA

WESTERN PALESTINE

AMMON

Amman

Jordan River

Jericho

Jerusalem

Azeqa

JUDAH

Beth Sur

Tell ed Duweir

Halhul

Gaza

Hebron

Tell Beit Mirsim

Dead Sea

Arnon River

MOAB

The Lisan

Ader

Kerak

Kurnub

EDOM

ARABA

TRANSJORDAN

Petra

Hamr Ifdan

Khirbet Nahas

Gharandel

ARABA

50 STATUTE MILES

Meneïya

Ain Defiya

SOUTHERN PALESTINE

AND

Ezion Geber

Gulf of Aqaba

Aqaba

TRANSJORDAN

descended from a height of about 2,700 feet above sea level to the Dead Sea Valley, which is 1,292 feet below sea level, the lowest point on the world's surface. After crossing the Allenby Bridge over the Jordan we began to go up into the hills of Ammon, and in the City of Amman (which the Greeks called Philadelphia) we picked up the other members of our expedition, Mr. R. G. Head and a remarkable Arab policeman named Ali Abu Ghosh.

Ali was assigned to us as a guard, but since there was never any guarding to do, he chose to assist us in our archaeological interests. Thus, among many other things, he learned from us the highly technical chronology of practically all of the ceramics of Palestine and Transjordan.

Another Arab, Hasan, joined our party. Though Hasan is one of the most arrant liars I have ever come across, I shall always think of him as an engaging companion. He had told us he had an intimate knowledge of the country we were going to traverse, although really he knew practically nothing about it. Fortunately, as things turned out, we did not need his advice on topographical matters. What Hasan could do to perfection was bake bread, and every day we enjoyed the unleavened native bread that he baked on a convex sheet of metal set on a tripod of stones over a blazing fire of desert thorns and twigs.

From Amman we drove on to Kerak, the Biblical city of Qir-Moab, a remarkable place on an isolated hill. The chief of police there assured us he would do everything to facilitate our expedition. We were to explore wild territory and we happily hired a sheikh called Auda, to supply us with camels and to guide us. The sheikh was called into the office of the police chief and was told that if anything should happen to any of us, he and his tribe would be held responsible. The best guarantee of safety in the desert is to be under the protection of a member of some influential tribe. Then no one in the desert will dare rob or kill the stranger because it is a part of honor for the protecting tribe to exact blood revenge.

Auda took with him four young men of his tribe to serve as camel boys. We hired five of Auda's camels at the high price of one dollar per camel per day. The camels were equipped with two goatskins used as water bags, one hanging on the left and one on the right side of each camel. Our sleeping bags were put over the rough wooden saddles, and the expedition was ready to start. I have a great affection for both the camel and the Bedouin, who go together perfectly in the desert. They live a sort of symbiotic existence, and it is almost inconceivable to think of the Bedouin Arab and his camel living independently in the Arabian Desert. For one thing the camel can do without water for days on end, and for another, the Arabs can find water where other men would die of thirst. It may just be a trickle, but they know where it is if it exists in their territory, and their territory is wide. No fodder need be taken along, for the ordinary camel can subsist on the sparse briars and thistles of the desert. At night the Arab lets his camel graze but the camel is hobbled to keep him from straying too far.

It has been said that the Arab is a parasite that lives on the camel, and this to a great extent is true. It is the camel that carries him about; it is the camel's hair that supplies him with both his clothes and his tent; the camel's dung is the fuel of the desert; it is the camel's meat that supplies food for his banquets; the camel's milk is his beverage; and I could go on enumerating the basic gifts of the camel to his Arab master.

Once our caravan was organized, we rode down toward the Dead Sea, specifically toward the "tongue" of land called the Lisan (Arabic for "tongue") that protrudes into the southern part of the Sea. As we descended we were on the look-out for two types of ruins. The first type is known as a tell. A tell is generally a mound consisting of several towns superimposed, one on the other. Tells arise when a town wall keeps the debris from being washed out by the rains. The other type of ruin is called a khirba. The latter has no wall roundabout to retain the soil and therefore the ruins are washed clean and exposed by the rains.

The terrain we were going to explore is called the Araba: the straight valley several miles across, extending from the southern end of the Dead Sea to the Gulf of Aqaba. We were undertaking this exploration during the finest of the seasons of the year, the spring. The rains were just ending and the desert was actually in flower. Though it may sound strange, there are about two weeks in the spring when the desert is a garden of yellows, blues, reds, and all the colors of the rainbow. The closest thing to romance that I have ever seen in the desert is a camel boy picking a beautiful bouquet of flowers and giving it most affectionately to his camel. The Bedouins have an extensive knowledge of plants and animals; and, among other things, know the camel's favorite flowers and weeds.

A few nomads were in the Araba at this time so that their goats and camels might graze on the seasonal vegetation of the desert. The inertia of tradition throughout the world, but especially there, is almost unbelievable. That was a famine year, and once, when we were passing by a stream full of trout and other tempting fish, these people were going with long-drawn faces, nearly starving to death. I asked them why they didn't catch and eat the fish. They said they couldn't; fish simply wasn't being eaten and they would rather starve. I asked if it was forbidden by their religion, and the reply was: no, nothing of the kind, it just wasn't being done. Their ancestors had come from the desert where fish do not exist and therefore are not eaten. Far be it from the Bedouins to depart from the ways of their fathers!

Our method of work was this: We rode along the foothills on either side, occasionally crossing the Araba in order to trace whatever ruins we could find including the old police posts that guarded the caravan trails in antiquity. The landscape is quite scenic, for both Eastern and Western Palestine are mountainous with the long, straight lane of the Araba between them.

Riding on a camel was a new experience. For the first

two or three days it was a bit trying until our abdominal muscles became accustomed to the motion. I cannot think of anything more peaceful than riding in the desert after the motion of the camel has become the normal state. Then the rider can attain an enviable state of mind with his thoughts either in the desert or worlds away. The camel, like the horse, can be a noble or a base creature. There are nags and racers among both species. I must confess that we were stuck with nags. When we had hired the camels we were told they were the finest racing camels in the land. It turned out that we couldn't get more than three miles an hour out of them, unless they were frightened, in which case the madness of their wild course was more striking than the speed. It seems that only the Arabs can make the proper sounds the camel understands, and vice versa. A guttural growl from the one is immediately understood by the other.

On the second night out we ill-advisedly camped near the water supply. Of course, the mosquitoes came down on us by the thousand. Among the follies of my youth was a slight touch of hypochondria. Consequently I thought of malaria and took quinine. Two days later Dr. Glueck got a slight attack of alternating fever and chills. Two days to the hour after that, he was taken with a worse attack. None of us knew much about medicine, but, since I was the son of a physician, my colleagues generally regarded me as the closest available approximation to a doctor. Anyway, I diagnosed the case as the type of malaria that occurs every two days, and, by anticipating his attacks and taking a goodly dose of quinine a little before the attack was due, he came through unscathed. After that experience we never camped near the water supply again. Instead, after filling our goatskins we would ride on for a distance before stopping for the night.

We came to a site on the east side, called Hamr Ifdan. Here we found a ruin and, examining its contour, found it to be a fortress. The pottery roundabout could be dated to the time of Solomon and to the period immediately following, which is known as the age of the Divided Monarchy. We wondered why a wise man like Solomon had built a large fortress in such an out-of-the-way place. Near by we noticed a spring, but even so, why come down to the most God-forsaken country of the world in order to build a fortress and guard a little bit of a spring? During the next few days we found out why King Solomon was interested in keeping this district under control and guarding all the available water supply. For, as we shall soon see, much of Solomon's famed wealth came from the desolate Araba.

As the evening drew on we sat around the fire, discussed the work of the day, and had our supper. This night we were troubled more than previous nights with the most distressing groaning of camels. We asked Sheikh Auda what all the noise meant. He told us of a quaint Arab custom: A milch camel had to be milked every night and, in order to get the camel's attention off the milking, they used to drive a wooden peg into her nose. We told Auda please to do this a little bit before bedtime thereafter so that the worst of the noise might by then be over.

That night was a bright moonlit night. I was fast asleep when, for some reason or other, I awoke and there was a tremendous arch stationed over me. It was a camel with its front legs on one side of me and its rear legs on the other. There was nothing I could do. I could not even flee, imprisoned as I was in my sleeping bag. I just waited and when the camel decided to go to another spot for grazing, he stepped across me and left me to my dreams.

The next important site we reached is known as Khirbet Nahas, which means the "ruin of copper." This was different from other places we had visited. Here we found hundreds of stone furnaces and beside them, heaps of slag. Obviously metal-bearing stones had been smelted here. We looked about us and found there were copper mines all about. Of course the next thing we did was to examine the abundant pottery lying around the furnaces. The sherds could be dated to the period of Solomon and his immediate successors: the same period as the Megiddo strata of Solomonic days and of a piece with the pottery we had found at Hamr Ifdan. Here were Solomon's mines so famed in literature; and for the first time in history mines were discovered that could definitely be attributed to Solomon on solid archaeological evidence. Perhaps it would have sounded a little more exciting had we found gold mines. However, it turns out that Solomon was a "copper king," and all along the Araba, on both sides, we found many copper mines and smelting stations, all attributable to Solomon and his immediate successors.

As we made our way southward, we came to a little oasis called Gharandel, which stays in my mind particularly because of a few welcome palm trees there. It was used in Nabatean and Roman times as a caravanserai and police post.

Crossing to the other side of the Araba, we came to the most scenic place I have ever seen in Western Palestine. (Most of the finest Palestinian scenery, like the Arnon Gorge and Petra, happens to be on the eastern side.) Our caravan entered this mountainous place called Meneïya at sunset. The coloring was superb. Within an hour or two we had discovered seven different mining and smelting sites, all datable to Solomon and the kings that followed him.

On the next day we went in a southeast direction, heading toward Aqaba, the city on the northeast corner of the Gulf of Aqaba. On the way we came to a well, known as Ain Defiya. The water there was brackish and so can be drunk without risk. However, it is salty enough to be quite unpalatable. We made tea out of it because we couldn't stomach it as it was. We put in lump after lump of sugar but to no avail. After drinking this unsavory tea and eating our lunch, I remarked to Hasan, "Tomorrow we shall be in Aqaba." He looked at me somewhat outraged and said, "Please don't say that. Say: Inshallah ['If Allah has willed it'], we shall reach Aqaba tomorrow." I thereupon asked why it was necessary to be so theological about such a commonplace, to which

Hasan replied: "Who knows, perhaps Allah has fore-ordained that this very night we shall be murdered and in the morning found lying in pools of our own blood." Afterwards I regularly prefaced "Inshallah" to all statements about future events. If one must speak with certainty, it is well to do so only in the case of past events for "the future is in the hands of Allah." And, I might add, the only way to gain peace of mind in a country of that type is to have the purely fatalistic attitude that goes with the land. None of us, not even Ali, could defend himself if we had been attacked during the night, for all of us were imprisoned so to speak in sleeping bags, from which we could not spring to our feet. Furthermore, we did not even ask Auda to have his lads take turns at standing guard during the night. Instead, we merely put our trust in Allah, for all men, but especially those that wander in His desert, are in His care.

At Aqaba we were received in the most hospitable manner of the Arabs. We were put up in the police station there. The prisoners, oddly enough, were walking about enjoying apparent freedom. They were used as waiters and servants instead of being shut up in cells. The police would say to them, "Won't you please do this or that?" and I could detect no trace of bullying or even of discourtesy to the prisoners.

On the first night a great feast was prepared for us. An Arab feast is something to remember. The guests sit in a circle and the food is brought in, in a large basin. The classical dish is a bed of rice with milk sauce, with either a roasted lamb or kid served on top of the rice.

Your host stands over you and occasionally picks the choice bits, like the liver, which he breaks into pieces and tosses graciously before you; you in turn nod to him, pick them up, and eat them. There are no spoons or forks or knives; no chairs or tables. The technique is quite simple but requires a good bit of delicacy. You take a fistful of the rice and squeeze it gently until the extra sauce drips out; then you open your mouth wide and toss the "bullet" of rice in, without getting any on your face. If you can do that, you have one of the essentials of "good table manners." There is no table talk. You are supposed to eat as quickly as you can and get full as soon as possible, because if you talk you are keeping others waiting. Then, to show you have had enough, you indulge in a lusty belch and rise to your feet. Servants then come with water, soap, and towel. You rinse your mouth, wash your face and hands, and sit on the side upon a comfortable divan and smoke a water pipe. Then the conversation begins. As you chat, your host will sprinkle rose water on you and sometimes ask you to hold out your hands so that he may pour some on them. The men of the place then sit about the same basin of food and have their fill. What they leave is taken out to the womenfolk and children. The status of woman is not high in modern Islam. In a later chapter (VIII) we shall show that she was far better off in certain bygone ages.

The next day we wanted to freshen up a bit and so made for the Gulf shore. Except for the jellyfish which had been washed up, the swimming was perfect.

We noticed not far north of the shore a mound in the middle of the Araba which rather surprised us, because the winds coming down from the north are generally strong and it would have been much more reasonable to build a city on either side of the Araba. This mound is called Tell Kheleifa, later identified as Ezion Geber, the seaport of Solomon on the Red Sea, and Glueck's excavations subsequently showed that it had been built by Solomon and that the chief industry was smelting. The smelting furnaces were actually situated with their backs toward the north, whence the winds come. There are holes in the north walls to serve as flues so that the wind would come in directly. In other words, the fanning of the fire was automatically taken care of by the steady winds that sweep down the Araba. The riddle of the location was thus surprisingly but plausibly solved.

It is interesting to note that from a somewhat later period, in the third city (not the first built by Solomon), was found a jar with South Arabian letters incised. This is evidence of trade with the land of the Queen of Sheba, who according to the Bible narrative had visited King Solomon. Her long trip to Jerusalem would doubtless have had business as well as personal motives.

After resting up a few days in Aqaba, we decided to go to Jebel Ramm. We were to motor this time. Our truck had come through by road over the mountains of Moab and Edom to meet us. We motored up through Wady Yitm to the plateau of the Arabian Desert. There nothing relieves the bleak wasteland except mirage. Usually the mirage lakes disappear when one approaches where they seem to be. Some in this district, however, seemed just as real as any lake even at very close range. It was like riding through a sea without splashing. Real objects like rocks and hills are reflected in mirage just as in genuine water. After riding through miles and miles of desert, we rubbed our eyes as if we had reached a fairyland, for ahead of us were bright purple mountains with cream-colored tops dazzling in the sun, all rising sheer out of a smooth plain. This time it was no optical illusion; we were in Jebel Ramm, the most fantastic landscape I have ever seen. There we found some of the Dominican Fathers excavating a Nabatean temple with beautiful painted columns. It was very pleasant to see the distinguished Fathers from Jerusalem uncovering the handsome Nabatean shrine.

After that we rode across the hilly, rocky fields of Edom and Moab, scanning the landscape for every ancient settlement. An examination of hundreds of sites showed that the countries were heavily occupied from the twenty-third to the nineteenth century B.C. Then there was a virtual blank with no occupied cities until the thirteenth century B.C. Now the historic importance of that is obvious to any Bible student because it is stated that the children of Israel wandered through that territory only to meet with opposition on the way to the Promised Land. Until the thirteenth century there could have been no such opposition because the land was devoid of a settled population. Therefore, the fifteenth century date of the Exodus that most scholars had been adhering to is quite out of the question, and we are obliged to return to the traditional date of the Exodus and Conquest in the thirteenth century.

From the thirteenth to the eighth century B.C. we found relics of a heavy period of occupation that terminated to a great extent early in the sixth century B.C. However, the richest period of all was the Nabatean age. The Nabateans developed their remarkable civilization especially during the first centuries before and after Christ and continued well into Roman times.

Interesting, too, is the fact that from 1200 A.D. to 1900 A.D. the country was virtually unoccupied: a gap of seven hundred years. Just in our own twentieth century are people resettling the land in more than negligible numbers. For the older periods, from the twenty-third to the nineteenth and from the thirteenth to the sixth centuries B.C., we were able to trace the fortresses that guarded the boundaries on the north and south that separated the ancient kingdoms from each other and also the fortresses for keeping the desert nomads from raiding the settled nations of Transjordan. By charting the cities, we were able to make a series of historic maps showing the places of settlement in each period. For by examining the pottery on any given site you can tell during which periods it has been occupied. As a rule, if no remains from a given period are found, the place was not occupied then. Not less than five hundred sites were occupied during the Nabatean period. Nabatean pottery is one of the finest groups I have ever handled in the Near East. It is fine of texture and often painted and sometimes incised, with a great variety of designs.

The most famous and the most beautiful of the Nabatean sites is Petra, which a modern poet has described as "the rose-red city, half as old as time." You come into it through a narrow gorge at the end of which you behold the most exquisite of a great series of buildings carved out of purple mountain sides with façades in handsome Hellenistic style. Inside, the rooms are carved out of the solid mountain walls. On both sides of the valley stand the magnificent buildings facing one another. It defies description. It is the sort of thing you have to visit to appreciate in all its majesty. If Jebel Ramm is the most beautiful landscape I have ever witnessed, Petra is the loveliest combination of art and nature.

I engaged a guide in Petra not so much for the misinformation that most guides are able to supply, but because he was an amusing fellow and because you can pick up quite a bit about the country and dialect from such guides. We came to a columbarium containing pigeon holes where the sacred doves used to roost. I asked him what it was and he replied it was an ancient postoffice, each hole being a "P.O.B." "That is very interesting," I said, "but how could anyone possibly get to those topmost boxes, which are several times higher than any man can reach?" Without hesitation he exclaimed, "Don't you know that in antiquity giants were in the land; each one forty cubits high?"

In addition to covering the Transjordanian or eastern part of the territory south of the Dead Sea we wanted to survey also the western, and, for that reason, we took

another short expedition from Jerusalem, later in the
summer. We went down to Beer Sheba, and down to the
Araba via Kurnub. The temperature was about 130 degrees in the shade with no shade to be had, and yet it
was not very uncomfortable because there was practically no humidity.

We had maps with us made by the British around the
time of the first World War. These maps naturally had
the wells and springs charted. We were depending on
finding a certain well, only to discover that it had dried
up since the map had been made. Two others that we
were looking for had also dried up in the meanwhile.
By that time we were in desperate need of water, for
we had but little water left in our canteens. We had told
our Greek truck driver to wait for us farther south, high
up on the mountains and not to try to meet us in the
impassable Araba. We held a "council of war" and wondered whether our water would enable us to meet the
driver at the top of the mountains. We decided that if
Allah was very, very kind to us, it might possibly be
done but things looked bad indeed. As we walked grimly
on our way through the desert one of our Arab camel
boys heard something. He leaped up on top of our bag-
gage camel (our only camel on this trip) and saw a most
welcome sight about a quarter of a mile away.

Our truck driver had disobeyed his orders, but had
used his intelligence, and blazed a trail which had never
been attempted by motor before. He had come down
with a truck full of supplies including plenty of water.

The day was saved. We shouted for joy, emptied our canteens down our parched throats, and ran to the truck to bless the disobedient driver and to drink our fill of water.

On our way back we went through the deserted regions of Sinai and southern Palestine. That entire country is now desolate except for a few nomads with their tents and flocks. Yet in the Byzantine period, part of it was full of men; men sought out that sequestered land as a retreat in which they might escape the evils of this world. Renouncing civilization, these men formed extensive monastic communities in the remote tracts of southern Palestine. Perhaps the most impressive of these settlements is Sbeita, excavated by the Colt Expedition. The excavators cleared out one of the ancient cisterns, and a few of the winter rains sufficed to fill the cistern with enough water to supply the expedition with water for the whole season. This illustrates the possibilities of almost any country, provided the right kind of people are there. With energetic people, the few, but heavy, winter rains can be stretched a long, long way.

Unfortunately the prosperity established by the Byzantines was effectively terminated by the Arab conquest. The Bedouin Arab is at home in the desert and can subsist and live his noble life of freedom in places where the Byzantine monk would have perished of thirst. But, on the other hand, the Bedouin is neither a builder nor cultivator. Under him, cisterns fill up and fertile terraced fields fall into ruin and become as the wilderness from which he emerged and in which he finds himself at home. And so today the southern wastelands of Palestine and Sinai are once more part of the far-flung terrain of the nomadic Semite, who roves as a herdsman, partaking of Allah's hospitality.

CHAPTER II

A MINOR EXPEDITION AMONG
THE "LIONS" OF ADER

AN ANCIENT site discovered in the course of exploration may be of sufficient interest to occasion trial sound-
ings before a major expedition is decided on. Also, some
ruins are of such limited size that a minor expedition of
a few weeks, or even days, is enough to realize the
objective.

In 1924, a group of American scholars, including Professor William F. Albright, visited in the course of their
expedition the site of Ader in Transjordan. What particularly attracted their attention was a temple which
had been built on the bedrock of a hilltop. The temple
dated from about 2000 B.C. and deserved excavation at
the earliest possible opportunity. Those scholars who
first visited the site also noted traces of the Early and
Middle Bronze Age, showing that it had been settled
before and after 2000 B.C., as well as traces of the Iron
Age of about 1000 B.C., and of Nabatean-to-Early
Arabic occupations.

In November, 1933, Dr. Albright organized a small
expedition to Ader. We left Jerusalem, went down across
the Jordan and up into the hills of Ammon and then into

the land of Moab, where Ader is situated. It was found that great changes had taken place since 1924. For one thing, the population of the town had quadrupled. Over the later ruins, a large Christian colony had settled and built, in addition to many private dwellings, a large church. It was an especially great disappointment to us to find that a group of nomads had settled on and around the top of the temple and had destroyed much of the ancient structure by using it as a quarry for getting stone to build their present houses. The home of the sheikh, for instance, was located squarely upon the temple. The sheikh was kind enough to let us dig through his courtyard to facilitate our study of what was left of the temple.

Our expedition was to last only about two weeks and we were operating on rather slender funds. We managed to rent a two-room wing of the church as quarters for the expedition. We used the smaller room for spreading out our sleeping bags at night, while the larger room served as our museum, workroom, storeroom, dining hall, and living room. We brought with us all the tools necessary for the digging and recording. The members of the expedition were few but willing; and I may say that the smaller the staff of an expedition the more important it is to have people who are good sports and who will not object to tasks they had not bargained for. Everyone must help in any way he can. For instance, I was one of the two cooks for the expedition, and that was a chore that I have never had to do either before or since. Two of the younger members of the staff shared the photographic work. All of us took part in the actual supervising of the laborers.

The Nabatean-to-Early Arabic ruins are situated, as we have already observed, in the part of the town now inhabited by the Christians. Dr. Albright, the director, supervised most of that part of the excavation himself. I was assigned to the work on the older period, across the wady. This area is now inhabited by Moslems of Bedouin stock, from whom we mustered about fifty sturdy men for excavating a couple of limited tracts.

Trial trenches are unfortunately a necessary aspect of "trial digs." As we shall see, in a major expedition the excavator proceeds level by level without pits. Pits and trenches often play havoc with a site and it is usually impossible to determine precisely the level of objects found in pits or trenches. Some excavators still try to justify pit sinking in principle. However, most archaeologists resort to clearing stratum after stratum if not over a whole site, then at least in a good-sized area. At Ader, where we had little time and money at our disposal, we were obliged to limit ourselves to small excavation areas which were methodically cleared down to bedrock.

I thus supervised the digging of a "sample area" measuring ten by four meters, and it proved to contain the remains of three different periods. The latest was 2000-1800 B.C., that is, in the transition from Early Bronze to Middle Bronze. Beneath, the preceding stratum had been destroyed by fire, for it was found covered with ashes. Below that, and on bedrock, was the earliest level of about 2300-2100 B.C. The evidence for dating the levels was almost entirely ceramic; numerous potsherds of well-known types settled the approximate chronology beyond cavil.

Thus while I supervised the Bronze Age area, Dr. Albright and the others were clearing a portion of the Nabatean-to-Early Arabic town across the wady. Dr. Albright also spent some time, with the assistance of other members of the staff and some of the natives, in making as exact plans as possible of the ill-fated temple.

Ader is a town completely unknown in the literature that has come down to us, so that whatever we found was in the nature of an addition to historical knowledge, and not merely a confirmation of it.

An unusual situation developed while I was completing my job of excavating the trial area. Our Sheikh Mohammed, a very valuable man who acted as my assistant foreman, asked me one day what we were trying to accomplish by digging; why were we spending good money to find old potsherds and bricks and fragmentary walls. I called him aside and said, "Sheikh Mohammed, you are an intelligent man and I speak to you as such. We are looking for traces of early civilizations—for things belonging to ancient men whom Allah has destroyed." "Ah!" said he surprised, "Ah! But why did you not tell me it was *that* you wanted? Had you told me, I could have showed you where the tombs of the Kings of Moab are." On hearing this, I was frankly startled, for we were in the heart of the land of Moab. Of course my better judgment dictated skepticism, but yet there is always the one chance in a million that oral tradition may reflect fact and may bring it to light by the oddest accident. I asked Mohammed what evidence he had for his assertion, and he said, "Do you see the mouth of that cave over there? Well, often have I seen fire like a streak of lightning issuing from that cave. That can mean nothing but that the kings of Moab lie buried there." (That, by the way, is a perfect example of an Arab syllogism.) I asked him if others had seen the same fire, and he said, "Yes, you may ask any of my brethren here. They will tell you, for they have seen the same thing." I called over a few of them—I do not think they had previously discussed this as a possibility for further digging—and they told me they had often seen the same fire. After lunch I told Dr. Albright about the amazing report, whereupon he walked across the wady with me to question the Arabs and examine the cave. He was as fascinated by the story as I had been. From what we could make out, it appeared that the flooring of the cave would date from the very earliest period that had come to light in our completed excavation—that is, from about 2300-2100 B.C. There was nothing to lose and everything to gain, and so we began work on the cave.

The cave had been filled up in antiquity and so we had to clear the entrance of the cave to the bedrock before we could dig inside. Mohammed reclined on the ground next to me, exhorting the men in their work. It was not, at that stage, delicate work: the pickmen would break the soil, which the shovel men would then put into baskets that the boys would carry off to the dump. Of course, all the laborers were looking for antiquities in the soil, for every one found would mean *baksheesh* (i.e., tips). I remember that I was urging them along as usual, while Mohammed, beside me, encouraged them with cries of "Up, O my lads! Soon we shall find the tombs of the Kings of Moab!"

But next day, the men appeared disgruntled as they came to begin work at sunrise. They were willing to clear away the small amount of that which remained to be cleared outside the cave, but when I gave the order to the pickmen to strike into the cave, a great cry arose, "No, no, we cannot do it! We have thought it over during the night, and we quit." Thus, was I confronted with a strike; and at that, so early in the morning. I asked Mohammed what his men meant, and he said they had sat up all night discussing it and had decided that though they would face any mortal foe or any beast of the field for us, their dear employers, they would not under any condition face the shades of the dead. Since the cave tombs were undoubtedly inhabited by "jinn" and "afarit," it would be impossible for them to excavate the cave, Mohammed apologetically but firmly explained.

I knew I had to get them back on the job or lose face forever; so I assembled the group in a semicircle around me, and, in my best Arabic, delivered an oration which ran something like this: "My men, I have come to you from across the seven seas, from the land of the Christians. Some day I shall go back whence I have come. There come times in the life of every man when he must decide what he will be like—whether he will be like unto the mouse, or like unto the lion." (They love to hear about animals; they are a naïve people, and one can appeal to them in ways that seem strange to us.) Then I went on with a glowing description of what the lion is like: how this courageous beast sallies from his den; how all the earth trembles at the sound of his voice; how he is respected above all the beasts of Allah's creation whereas the weak mouse must flee at the sight of even a cat, and lives his wretched life in constant fear. I concluded: "And now, decide whether you are like unto the lion or like unto the mouse!" A few cried out, "We are like the lion, O Khawaja, we are like the lion!"; but most still maintained a silence dictated more by confusion than discretion. Then I went on with another glamorous account of the exploits of the lion, and told them that the time had come to make up their minds. By this time they had been fanned into a state more akin to frenzy than mere enthusiasm, and they shrieked out their decision to be like lions. Quickly seizing the opportunity, I said: "All right, you have made up your minds, you are lions. And do you not know where the lion has his home? Is it not *in the cave?*" To my relief and joy many men got up at once and took up their picks. "My lions, dig!" I shouted, and the work went on. There were still about ten "mousy" men on the sidelines, but, fortunately, within a few minutes five or six of them came up to me and said they had reconsidered matters and would rather be lions than mice, so I reinstated them. Gradually, all but one had joined the lions, and I am sorry to say that I gave the lone mouse an unkind look and taunted him by saying, "So you are the mouse; run away then, before my lions devour you!" Whereupon the other men growled and jumped at him. At last, with tears in his eyes, he said that he too would try to be a lion if he were only given another chance. Magnanimously I elevated him from mousedom to lionhood, and thus all of my strikers were won back to their jobs—with no increase in pay nor decrease in hours. All they had needed was the heart of a lion. They worked as I have never seen men work before or since. As they dug away, Mohammed and I kept encouraging them with cries of, "Who are you?" to which they would call back, "We are your lions!" We found, as we had foreseen, remains of occupation from the twenty-third to the twenty-first centuries B.C.; and while what we unearthed was unspectacular, with no vestige of the tombs of the kings of Moab, it represented a very gratifying return for the few days we put in.

On next to the last day, when the men were sealing the entrance to the cave with rocks so that illicit diggers could have no easy access to it in our absence, Sheikh Yusuf, the sheikh of sheikhs in that district, passed by on his journey through his territory, and as he drew near on his white mare, he heard the men cry "We are your lions!" He accordingly asked Mohammed, "What mean these words I hear?" Mohammed proudly replied, "Have you not heard? The Khawaja has come across the seven seas to pick my tribe out of all the tribes of Islam to be the Tribe of the Lions." I did not want to miss any of this conversation, so I blew my whistle for time out, and joined Mohammed and Yusuf. I put in a good word for

Mohammed to his superior, informing Sheikh Yusuf that I had been entertained by sheikhs and emirs from Cairo to Baghdad and from Istanbul to Arabia, and never had I met a man as worthy as Sheikh Mohammed to be called the Sheikh of the Lions. Mohammed beamed and bowed in gratitude. A large crowd had gathered to see our distinguished visitor. As I was about to blow my whistle to resume work, Mohammed asked for one more minute, and waving his hands dramatically, cried, "Hear, you rabble! From this time on, you shall call my tribe, not the Tribe of Such-and-Such but the Tribe of the Lions; nor let any of you address me as Sheikh Mohammed, but from now on as Mohammed, the Sheikh of the Lions. Now, get away!" Thus had I innocently changed the name of a tribe in Moab and thus had I conferred a new title on a tribal chieftain.

CHAPTER III

SITES OF SIMPLE STRATIFICATION

FEW MOUNDS consist of only one level, and even fewer consist of one level without sub-phases. One of the most beautiful examples of a simple site is Khorsabad, built by Sargon of Assyria and completely abandoned at the end of his reign. It is a beautiful capital, with a city wall, temples, a palace filled with sculptures of winged bulls and other colossi; and painted tile murals. It includes a ziggurat, or stage tower, that formed part of the buildings of the religious complex; and perhaps most significant, from it there came to light a tablet bearing a list of the kings of Assyria from the third millennium B.C., down to the Sargon who built Khorsabad. Historians await impatiently the publication of this precious document.

Another famous capital occupied for only one generation is Tell el Amarna, built by the Pharaoh Ikhnaton and completely abandoned soon after his death. We shall hear more of Tell el Amarna in another connection.

It is interesting that in Egypt the situation is in general quite different from that in Western Asia. The settlements were in the Nile Valley, but the Nile bed is constantly rising, and therefore there has been a continual abandonment of sites which ultimately come to lie under the water level, while the new villages spring up at a safer distance from the advancing shore. Perhaps some day the Nile at certain points may be deflected from its present course, and epoch-making excavations will be undertaken. But things being what they are, there are practically no known mound sites or stratified cities available for excavation in Egypt.

The most simply stratified site (at least architecturally) that I have ever helped excavate is the Judean fortress, Beth Sur.

The history of this Judean fortress is known from literary sources. In Joshua we read that the district including Beth Sur was overrun by the tribe of Judah, at approximately 1200 B.C. From Chronicles, we learn that Rehoboam refortified the city. In the second century B.C., known as the Maccabean period of Jewish history, we know both from First Maccabees and from Josephus that Beth Sur was a great garrison town, second in importance only to Jerusalem. In the Maccabean period we find the following scheme of events: About 165 B.C. Judas Maccabeus with 10,000 followers routed 65,000 of the Greco-Syrian troops of Lysias. Judas Maccabeus and his brothers were thus enabled to restore and rededicate the Temple—an event still celebrated each December by the Jewish people as the Feast of Lights. Also, almost immediately thereafter, Beth Sur was refortified by Judas. The Asiatic wing of Alexander's empire had been left to the house of Seleucus. The Seleucids persecuted the Jewish nation, which still retained its old fighting spirit. The Jews were a little people but, prompted by the noble instinct to be free, preferred death to submission.

Lysias later came back to Beth Sur with the boy king Antiochus V, but the people sallied forth and burned his engines of war. Lysias and Antiochus were forced to leave the town because Judas Maccabeus was carrying on the war in another part of the country. But the Judeans later lost the fortress to Antiochus V because the Greco-Syrians resorted to the following strategy: It was a Sabbatical (or seventh) Year, during which debts must be remitted, Hebrew slaves set free, and the land allowed to lie fallow. For the last reason, the food supplies were low; but rather than disobey the laws of their fathers, the Jews chose to face the consequences of the serious food shortage which finally obliged them to surrender the town, from which they were then sent forth naked. The general Bacchides was left in charge of the garrison. Not long afterwards, however, Judas' brother Simon recaptured the city and converted it into a Judean town again. Such, in outline, is the history of Beth Sur as far as it was known from written records.

The first problem of the archaeologist was to identify that city with the proper modern site. From the Bible we know that Beth Sur is in the Hebron district near the settlement of Halhul. The latter place is known and the modern village there still bears the same name.

In the Halhul district there is the mound of a large walled town; the Arabs call it Khirbet et Tubeiqa. (It has been called a khirba rather than a tell because part

of the ruins remained exposed throughout the centuries.)
An examination of the surface sherds showed at once
that the place had been heavily occupied in the Hellenistic Age including the Maccabean period. There were
also traces of the earlier settlements that are indicated
for Beth Sur in the historical records. Thus Khirbet et
Tubeiqa fulfilled the indispensable requirements of an
identification: to wit, the (1) locational (near Halhul),
(2) descriptive (a large walled town) and (3) archaeological (traces of the right periods of occupation). On
the other hand, (4) traditional evidence was lacking:
i.e., the present inhabitants did not know that Khirbet
et Tubeiqa marks the site of Beth Sur, as they happen,
for instance, to know that modern Khalil marks the site
of ancient Hebron. Nor was there (5) direct toponymic evidence; for the modern name (Khirbet et Tubeiqa), is not the same as Beth Sur (contrast "Halhul,"
where the old name has survived unchanged). The absence of traditional and toponymic evidence does not
necessarily invalidate an identification. It is interesting to
note that in this case there is some significant, though
indirect, toponymic evidence. A Byzantine fortress situated quite close to Khirbet et Tubeiqa, bears the name
of Burj es Sur—meaning "The Tower of Sur." Thus the
name of the old city has been partly preserved in that of
the Byzantine tower. Accordingly, there is striking,
though indirect, toponymic evidence for the identification of Khirbet et Tubeiqa with Beth Sur. It will be
seen that the excavation of the site in 1931 confirmed
the identification.

We undertook the excavation during the summer months when there is no rainfall. Accordingly we were able to live in tents. We engaged about 150 laborers. While their salaries were not high, as a rule we used to give them generous *baksheesh* for any antiquities that they would find and report immediately and remove without damage. This was an incentive for them to keep their eyes wide open, to work carefully, and to turn in everything they found.

The method of digging (of which we shall have more to say) was, in brief, the clearing of the debris down to the floor level, making accurate notations as to the provenance of every article found, then labeling it adequately; entering these records in the books, and making sure that all the objects and buildings discovered were photographed and drawn; in other words, taking precautions to keep definite and detailed records of what we found so that a scientific account might be published for the entire scholarly world. Actually the preliminary report by Professor Ovid Sellers, who directed the expedition, is a model publication.

Excavation showed that the people who built the fortress in the Hellenistic period went down to bedrock, destroying most of the remains of the older periods; therefore, we found virtually no architecture other than the well-preserved Hellenistic level of the second century B.C. This appeared to be divided into three building phases, which are perhaps to be correlated with the known building operations of Judas, Bacchides, and Simon. The debris of the earlier periods had been used for filling in at various places so that the traces of many different ages were mixed. We found some sherds from the Early Bronze Age; more from about 1800 to 1550 B.C.; and a large number of Israelite sherds reflecting the occupations down to the time of Nebuchadnezzar. These mixed finds show what stress must be laid on ceramics, for if we had not known Palestinian pottery, we would have thought that many relics of remote antiquity were Hellenistic because they happened to be found with Hellenistic remains. The confusion had resulted simply because the Hellenistic builders were too thorough (from the archaeologist's viewpoint) and went down to bedrock for laying the foundations of their fortress. The true identification of all these mixed potsherds and other relics had to be based on a knowledge of the previous discoveries at well-stratified Palestinian sites.

Practically all the walls were made of stone, so that the ground plans were easy to trace. If wall stones are in place, it is comparatively easy to remove the dirt and fallen stones from around them, and so the wall emerges. To be exact, only the lower parts and the foundations emerge, for usually the roof and upper parts have long since collapsed. We found that the city included fortifications, city gates, market places, shops, and private dwellings. One house contained tubs, but we were not sure whether they were for bathing or dyeing. There was no trace of color left in the tubs, but dyes might fade in the course of the two millennia that separate us from the Maccabeans.

Several of the shops were obviously wine shops. The

Greco-Syrian soldiers (rather than the Judeans) may have imported wine from the Island of Rhodes; for there were a great number of stamped wine-jar handles showing that the jars came from Rhodes. The stamps sometimes bear the names of the potters; the names of the Rhodian officials known as Eponyms, after whom the years were named; and sometimes the Rhodian month is written as well.

Among the miscellaneous discoveries was the grave of a man, presumably a soldier, whose spine had been violently broken just above the pelvis; so violently in fact that it is conceivable (though not demonstrable) he had been stepped on by one of the elephants used by the Seleucids in battle. One of the heroic Maccabean brothers was killed by an elephant on the battlefield according to First Maccabees, and other soldiers doubtless met their death that way.

The site was well equipped with cisterns for holding water, which was important particularly during sieges. We found one great reservoir with two entrances, of which the smaller was outside the city wall. It had probably been at first a natural pocket in the rock and was then improved by hewing. The Judeans may have made their sortie against the soldiers of Lysias by getting out of the smaller entrance. In this large reservoir we found many kinds of bones mostly of animals but some of men; the latter would seem to be evidence of foul play. We also found the jaw of an *asinus onager*, a wild ass that has since become extinct. Thus archaeological research may prove of interest for many fields of investigation, even to the zoologist and the palaeontologist.

The danger of being a mere armchair archaeologist was illustrated by an incident at Beth Sur. A distinguished library archaeologist who had never been a member of an expedition, visited our excavations. We were showing him the reservoir, into which the yearly winter rains keep seeping, so that the debris is kept wet from year to year. He looked at the wet floor of the reservoir and asked of what period the reservoir was. We replied it was of the Maccabean period. "The Maccabean period—wonderful!" he exclaimed. "And the water is still here!"

Another amusing incident in that campaign bears repetition: After working hours I used to wrestle on an extra tent flap with our sturdy photographer. The venerable mukhtar (or mayor) used to watch us intently evening after evening. One day Professor Albright said to him, "O Mukhtar Yusuf, what do you think of the American sport of wrestling?" Yusuf shook his head and said, "The art of wrestling doubtless comes from Allah and all of Allah's works are good; but, Khawaja Albright, would it not be more effective if they used daggers?"

From the period called Early Iron II (that is, from about 900 to 600 B.C.) we found several jars with stamps that showed they had been used to contain taxes paid to the king. They read: "To the King: Hebron" (that is, from Hebron); "To the King: Ziph"; "To the King: Mamshat."

We found many Egyptian scarabs, of types which

could be correlated with the well-known dynasties of Egypt. We found also various stone weights with their Hebrew names inscribed on them; e.g. the "nesef," the "pym," the "beqa." Since these stones have not changed in weight we know to what weight the Hebrew words refer. These terms in Scripture are, so to speak, words rather than definite weights until you find the actual inscribed stones that tell what the word signifies in terms of weight. Archaeology provides, as it were, the illustrations for the modern edition of the Hebrew, Greek, Latin, and other classics. Beth Sur also yielded numerous coins, mostly from the Seleucids, who were Alexander's successors in Asia; many from the Ptolemies, Alexander's successors in Egypt; and quite a few from the valiant Maccabeans who shook off the yoke of the Greco-Syrian tyrants.

After these discoveries, there was no doubt as to the identification of Beth Sur: It had been confirmed up to the hilt.

CHAPTER IV

MOUNDS OF MANY CITIES

THE DEVELOPMENT of a science can often be traced in terms of the contributions of the pioneers who created it. We might well start with the name of P. E. Botta, a Franco-Italian archaeologist, who almost exactly a century ago began the science of mound excavation, at the Assyrian capital of Khorsabad. Nothing was then known of stratification: the whole idea of cities piled one on top of another was quite foreign to everyone. Fortunately for Botta, he picked one of the few sites in the Near East that are in the form of mounds and yet have no stratification.

In the years that followed, many distinguished men, among whom we may single out the British archaeologist Austen Henry Layard, entered on expeditions in several rich mounds including Nineveh, Nimrud, and Assur, the capitals of ancient Assyria. While pioneers such as Layard made many spectacular discoveries, they damaged and destroyed much of the evidence. Nor did Layard know that Nineveh and Assur were mounds of many cities. But Layard will be remembered for his splendid contributions and not for such shortcomings as are bound to accompany work in a new field.

Treasure hunting went on for quite a while, and it was Heinrich Schliemann at Troy who first recognized that he was dealing with superimposed cities.

The next great name is that of a living Englishman, Sir Flinders Petrie, who recognized the potential importance for dating purposes of small, insignificant-looking objects such as fragments of pottery. The attention he paid to details overlooked by other excavators enabled archaeology to make its greatest strides since Schliemann's discovery of stratification. But archaeology required rigid standards of exactitude before it could become the science it is today. Field technique has reached the highest existing standards under Professor George A. Reisner of Harvard University. Reisner's excavations are models of painstaking carefulness, and his records are characterized by a fullness that aims at perfection. He is still actively engaged in publishing his model works on Egyptian archaeology. Unfortunately, his sight has been failing him, and scholarship is lucky that his daughter is assisting him in producing the valuable publication of his discoveries. No amount of description is too much for Dr. Reisner; no number of photographs too great; no detail too minute to be recorded. His thoroughness has set a model that we all try to attain.

The men we have singled out are actually but a few of the many great names in the annals of the development of archaeology. However, they suffice for sketching the evolution of the subject. The age of treasure hunting is over, for it is no longer a legitimate form of archaeology. Instead of that, the discipline of the archaeologist now requires well-recorded, stratigraphic excavation. A site is excavated layer by layer, and what is found in each layer is recorded, photographed, planned and described. The value of stratigraphic excavation is best brought out by the fact that it has vastly widened the horizon that we had of human history a hundred years ago. We can now go back to perhaps the sixth millennium B.C., so that our knowledge of architecture, of art, of countless aspects of life, is now more than doubled—thanks to stratigraphic excavation. When I say "*perhaps* the sixth millennium," I am making a necessary reservation, because we have only relative chronology for the earlier periods: What lies underneath must be earlier than the layer above, but to give each layer an exact date is out of the question at present. In some cases it is possible to establish exact chronology for prehistoric periods. Thus by counting the annual rings of the yellow pine logs used in the Pueblos, one can establish an accurate chronology for periods unattested in written records. Or, again, one may base precise chronological schemes on layers of the Dead Sea basin, where successive years have left, each its lamination. However, we have not discovered any such device for an absolute chronology of the prehistoric settlements buried in the mounds of the Near East.

Before continuing our account, we might well ask ourselves why settlers chose a given place for building a city. In the Near East, as we have already observed, the chief necessity of life is water. Therefore, closeness to a

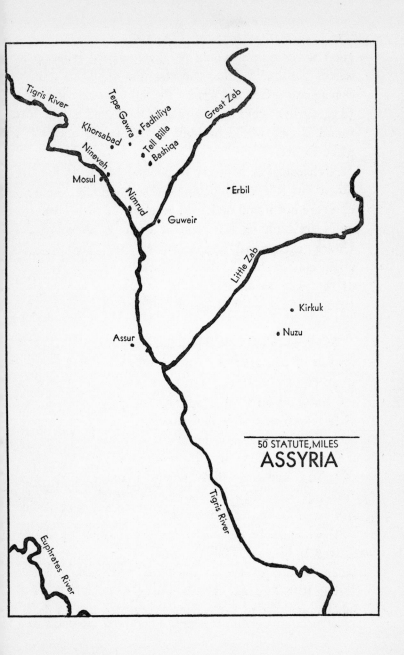

Tigris River

Tepe Gawra

Fadhiliya

Khorsabad

Great Zab

Tell Billa

Nineveh

Bashiqa

Mosul

Erbil

Nimrud

Guweir

Little Zab

Kirkuk

Nuzu

Assur

50 STATUTE, MILES

ASSYRIA

Tigris River

Euphrates River

good water supply would be an important criterion in selecting a site. Another consideration would be protection against attack and against the unkindnesses of nature (e.g., against wind and storms). Once such a spot was found, a city would be built by settlers in quest of a place to live.

Archaeologists, contrary to popular belief, do not dig down into the earth below the surrounding country; cities are not found under the level of the plain. Ancient cities are built on the plain or even on an eminence. Under exceptional circumstances, the archaeologist might conceivably dig down into the soil below the level of the plain to unearth tombs or cisterns. But in four years of field work, I never came across such a procedure.

The next question is: How did cities come to be piled on top of one another? Ancient cities sometimes came to an end by violent means; for example, destruction at the hands of an enemy. The bloodthirsty kings of Assyria record time after time that they came to such-and-such a city, captured it, burned it with fire and made of it a *tell*. These kings actually went about the destruction of cities knowing they would convert them into "mounds" and they use the same word that the Arabs still use to designate a "mound."

Towns may be demolished by the violence of nature as well as of men. Thus the walls of Jericho may have fallen because of one of the many earthquakes of the Jordan Rift. Fire may destroy a town so quickly that the inhabitants have to flee leaving everything behind them.

The Temple of Bacchus at Baalbek: an unusually fine example of the Hellenistic architecture that the Nabateans
adapted to the carving of cities like Petra out of mountain
walls.

The mound of Tepe Gawra, as viewed from the northwest, after the removal of the eight upper levels. Since the debris of the excavated towns has been dumped over the sides, the mound is considerably wider than it was before work began.

One of the most interesting discoveries I have ever witnessed in excavating a mound was a kitchen in an ancient house at Tepe Gawra, with the supper still on the fire —the lid still on the pot and the food still inside; the meat, of course, had disappeared during the centuries but the bones were there undisturbed. The house had burned down so quickly that the household had to abandon everything including the cooking dinner.

Sudden destruction by fire preserved Level VIII of Tepe Gawra in some places to a height of four meters. The conflagration burned the mud-brick walls into hard baked bricks, thus preserving them for the modern excavator. The misfortune of ancient man is often the good fortune of the archaeologist. When a town was destroyed by fire, the inhabitants had to leave everything behind them so that all the noninflammable objects are preserved in ashes for the lucky excavator. However, wherever the inhabitants had time to vacate without hurrying they would naturally take most of their possessions with them so that the archaeologist is the poorer. If we choose to be mathematical about it we might formulate the situation thus: the luck of the archaeologist is in inverse ratio to that of the ancient man. However, settlements do not always come to violent ends. The constant dumping of refuse tends to raise the street level, a process that can still be observed in existing communities of the Near East. I have been particularly impressed by this process as I saw it going on in Mosul. If much rubbish is thrown out of doors, the street level may rise as much as several feet in the course of a generation.

Then there is the phenomenon of rebuilding: When someone decides to replace his roof, the old roof may be thrown down onto the street, so that the latter rises appreciably and suddenly.

After a town is destroyed or abandoned, the surface tends to be leveled off more through the agency of the people who come to rebuild it than by dust or shifting sands. Jeremiah recognized this principle when he wrote: "And the city shall be rebuilt *on its tell*." He knew that the cities of Judah would be destroyed when Nebuchadnezzar was about to overrun the country; but he prophesied that, as before, their descendants would rebuild the Judean cities on their ancient mounds. He too uses the word *tell*, the word still in use in Arabic. But this principle remained unrecognized (and the Bible passage, misunderstood) by Occidental scholars till Schliemann's time, well on in the nineteenth century.

But why should people build on these ancient mounds? Well, it might be for sentimental reasons, because this had been the spot where they or their forefathers had lived. Or, more commonly, for practical reasons: If access to a source of good water had made the site worthwhile in the first place, why should it not be so again? Then too, the added elevation of the mound was advantageous, for height facilitates defense in case of attack, as well as both drainage in the rainy season and sewage disposal throughout the year.

At this point it would be well to distinguish between a *stratum* and a *phase*. A stratum is what remains of an occupation in which the structures are independent of those below and above. However, buildings are re-used to a considerable extent; and when old walls are appropriated by people living on new floor levels, the floor levels in question indicate phases of the same stratum. The keenness of the archaeologist in the field is judged not so much by his ability to distinguish strata as by acumen in distinguishing phases within the stratum. Sometimes there may be only ten or twenty years between an earlier and a later phase, and their identification may call for a good bit of subtlety.

As for the method of digging: In the first place, the archaeologist should start at the top of the mound. If, as is often the case, it is too large to excavate in its entirety, he should take as large an area as practicable, digging in it down to the floor level of each successive layer. To sink holes and dig trial trenches promiscuously only ruins a mound, and up-to-date archaeologists do not resort to such methods. Even attacking the mound from the side is not an approved method, for on the side the stratification is usually obscure. Ideally, the excavator should expose a whole level at once and then proceed downward, level by level, but in practice most mounds are too large for such a lengthy and costly procedure. The model big-scale excavation in the Near East is that undertaken at Megiddo by the Oriental Institute of the University of Chicago. If there had been any doubt in my mind as to the value of uncovering an entire city, that doubt was dispelled when I visited Megiddo and saw the complete Israelite city containing the now famous stables of Solomon. However, the Oriental Institute was able to undertake such a monumental project only because of the unusually large funds at its disposal. The depression years unhappily precluded the possibility of digging all the earlier Megiddo levels in their entirety. The singularly important early finds at Megiddo were made in limited areas of excavation.

Actually, stratigraphic excavation is not so simple as one might gather from the above generalizations. When one digs down to the ground level of a stratum and clears the entire stratum, he will usually meet with "intrusions" that extend below the floor of the stratum in question; as is the case with cellars, wells, cisterns, or graves. Furthermore, foundations are of necessity *under* the floor level to which they correspond. Intrusions are so important and interesting that a separate chapter (V) is devoted to them.

Both while the digging is going on, and also after the level is cleared with its ruined edifices still standing, a thorough study must be made. Exact notes must be made of the location and position of all the significant objects found, before they are removed for closer examination, for once a thing is removed from the soil, the evidence to be gathered from its context is lost. The field notes made in the course of the excavation are an important aspect of archaeological work. Delicate objects must be handled with special care and preserved by the best available methods. There is hardly such a thing as too full or too detailed a catalog; too many pictures; too numerous or too precise drawings or plans; too many field notes or too much care in exhuming and preserving antiquities.

Clearing a level is not usually an easy task. Thus, suppose you are unearthing a mud-brick building whose roof and upper walls have long since fallen down. How are you to tell the collapsed from the standing parts of the wall? It is almost a fine art in some cases to tell the difference between the wall proper and the fallen debris, but there are certain standard ways of detecting which is which. For instance, bricks are laid in level courses; therefore when an excavator finds, in cutting through an unbaked brick mass, slanting or broken lines of mortar, they tell him that the brick is not in place but constitutes fallen debris and is to be removed. However, if the lines of mortar are horizontal, the bricks form part of a standing wall which is to be spared and the debris cleared from around it. Walls are sometimes faced with a film of plaster and when this film is vertical it is in place. Otherwise it indicates fallen debris. However, when, as occasionally happens, the wall was made of one clay mass and not of bricks in courses, the excavator must beware of mistaking the debris on one side of the plaster for the wall on the other.

Eventually the whole level is uncovered by removing debris and baring the standing edifices. Pavements and floors are distinguished if not by a special finish, at least by a degree of hardness, from the filling above them. A pavement faced with stone is, of course, quite easy to detect. Once the street or floor level is struck, it is well to clear the entire stratum down to this level with great caution, for vases and other delicate objects will be found on the floor (not suspended in mid-air). Work with heavy tools such as picks should be suspended and the floors should be cleared and walls traced by skilled laborers employing gentle means.

As has already been mentioned, after a level has been bared it must be utterly demolished in order to find the stratum below it. The excavator must therefore be very careful, because once he removes a layer in order to get at the one below it, the evidence of the upper layer is destroyed for all time, and only his records of it survive. In other sciences, such as chemistry and physics, the same experiment can normally be repeated; if the material in one test tube is somehow confused, unobserved or destroyed, the material can normally be duplicated and the experiment repeated in another test tube. But archaeological evidence, which cannot be duplicated and yet must be destroyed, calls for the utmost restraint and patience and scientific conscience in the excavator.

It is well to say a word about people who should go into archaeological work—and about those who should not. Playboys should keep away. They do more damage than good. People who go out looking for a thrill, for the romance of the Orient and the glamour of antiquity, are more often than not liabilities to an expedition. After a month or two they tend to tire of the inescapable daily routine, and to long for a less exacting life. For people who have the necessary background and training, however, the work will have an enduring attraction. Speak to people who have done archaeological field work and you will note that in nearly every case they want to get back to excavating or exploring as soon as possible—not so much for the glamour of exotic places as because they like the work and the mode of life. Archaeological opportunity should only be offered to and accepted by trained people with a mature interest in the subject.

Many diverse talents may go into the making of a useful archaeologist. One may be an expert photographer, or an expert draftsman, or an expert at handling museum pieces. All these people have their place as specialists, under the leadership of the director who plans the work and correlates the findings of the expedition. Everyone on the dig, regardless of his specialization, tends to take some active part in the field work, assisting in supervising the workmen and making field notes. When something that looks interesting is found, one must be prepared to roll up his sleeves (if they are not rolled up already), take a knife, and dig the thing out himself. But more than anything else an understanding of the nature, purpose, and significance of the work is necessary, so that one's interest will make an expedition lasting six months or more be interesting every moment of the time.

Some people are by temperament unfitted for archaeological work. The person who comes to work in the morning, or sits down to a meal, with a scowl on his face, will not wear well especially during the rainy season. One must be good and solid as a human being, as well as technically equipped in some way. But if one is prepared and fit for it, I cannot think of a better way to spend one's life. Before ending this digression on personal fitness, we might note some distinctions so as not to leave too absolute an impression. Men with not quite enough stability for excavation may have the modicum for exploration, while men a trifle too finicky for the rigors of exploring may not be too much so for excavating. The climate, duration of the campaign, and proximity "to civilization" are among the many factors that should be considered when selecting members of the staff.

I shall illustrate stratigraphy from the excavations at three well-stratified sites: at Tepe Gawra and Tell Billa in Assyria near Nineveh and at Tell Beit Mirsim in Judea.

Before excavating a mound, one must secure the right to dig there. We were very fortunate in the case of Tepe Gawra, for it was the property of an enlightened Moslem of Mosul who donated it to the expedition for the sake of science. You often hear of Oriental avarice; but I have been more impressed by Oriental generosity. Indeed, Tepe Gawra, like Tell Billa, lies in a very fertile part of Iraq and is agriculturally profitable; and yet the owner of Tepe Gawra refused any monetary recompense. That simplified things immensely, for negotiations for the purchase or lease of mounds are often very difficult, not so much because of the money involved as because of certain human complications about which we shall have more to say.

Tepe Gawra was abandoned by the end of the fifteenth century B.C. because by that time the twenty-odd successive levels had gradually converged till the top came to a point capable of holding just one building:

a watch tower. Sheer want of space fixed the later limit of Gawra's remarkable record of the march of time.

The three uppermost levels belonged to the Hurrians, who have been becoming more and more important to the historian. They came into Mesopotamia in the second half of the third millennium and were a dominant ethnic element throughout the Near East during the second millennium B.C. It was through the Hurrians that Assyrian civilization affected the Hittites. Hurrians ruled the great Mitanni empire in the fifteenth and fourteenth centuries. Scholars in America and Europe have been making great strides in interpreting the cuneiform texts in the Hurrian language that have been unearthed in Egypt, Canaan, Anatolia, and Mesopotamia.

The sixth level (from the top) was made of stone and surrounded by a town wall. The artistic objects found therein, dated it to the period of the famous royal tombs discovered at Ur. So Level VI provided a fixed point for reckoning back in history. I might also add that Tepe Gawra, especially in the case of the upper half of the mound, was an acropolis rather than a complete city. Most of the people lived outside the walls and would take refuge inside only in times of siege. The municipal buildings, temples, and other important structures were within the walls, while most of the private dwellings lay outside.

Level VII had virtually no structures left but only pottery and small objects. When a level is without structures, it is usually because the foundations of the city above were laid with such thoroughness that the buildings in the layer below were destroyed. But Level VIII, fortunately for us, had been destroyed by fire, so that the walls were preserved to an unusual height; in one place (as mentioned above) to a height of four meters. Accordingly, such architectural features as windows and the true arch were attested for the first time in history. I do not mean to imply that they had never existed before this period, for certainly they must have come from somewhere, but every previous excavation of such antiquity had yielded only the nether parts of the walls and therefore all such architectural features had been destroyed.

We found many arrowheads of obsidian and flint at this level. Base metals were not yet in use, for this was around the middle of the fourth millennium before the Bronze and Iron Ages. We found a mace head of basalt pierced so that a shaft could be placed through the hole; the weapon was to be used on the enemy's head. We also found an arsenal: a room filled with clay slingshots. The inhabitants had thus been expecting some trouble such as eventually did befall them. In order to assure themselves of a water supply in time of siege they had constructed a reservoir dug through 20 meters of earlier citadels and into virgin soil. It must have been very difficult to construct; it was hard enough for us to clear. But in spite of all their military and strategic precautions, their city was devastated by fire and became a "story" in Tepe Gawra's skyscraper of history.

We found that Level VIII was divided into three phases. The difficulty of the subdivision of a stratum into phases is that, in a given period, some structures may be re-used while others are replaced. Thus a given occupation may be partly a phase of the preceding settlement and partly a new stratum. Such was actually the case in what we decided to call the "phases" of Level VIII.

Underneath the *a*, *b*, and *c* "phases" of Level VIII, we found the ground plan of a temple in Level IX. There was nothing primitive about it; it was symmetrical, well thought out, and well executed, and in its day must have been quite handsome. The façades, niches, and recesses and plastered surface added to its beauty.

Below, in a level we decided to call XI*a*, we found an entirely different school of architecture, represented by a round house with a very interesting and varied arrangement of the rooms. Whether this round house belonged to some regular "school" of architecture or whether it came into being on the site because the ancient architects decided to follow the circular contour of Tepe Gawra, we do not know. In no case does the student of Gawra's architecture complain of monotony.

Among the small finds in Level XI were many seal impressions. This was before the time of writing, and to indicate ownership personal seals were stamped on clay. An animal appearing frequently on these seals was the salugi. It is a dog of the greyhound type still common in the Near East. Fortunately for the salugi, it is not classed as a dog in Arabic. The dog is considered an unclean animal, and is tabu. Dogs are not to be taken into the house nor do the Arabs treat them as pets or companions. But the salugi is considered a different animal, just as we consider canines like the fox, jackal, or wolf as animals that are not dogs in the sense that poodles or spaniels are. So the salugi is kept in the house and fondled, clothed in winter, and is his master's companion especially while hunting. The Gawra seals throw the history of the salugi back to the fourth millennium B.C. in Assyria.

So far Tepe Gawra has been excavated to Level XVII. That is, seventeen distinct strata (not counting phases!) have been unearthed one below the other.

From Level XII to Level XVII the cities show a mixture of cultures, being a kind of blend of the earliest culture of southern Babylonia, known as the Obeid, and of the Halaf which precedes the Obeid in Assyria. Who knows, then, what is going to be found in the strata that remain to be excavated below Level XVII after this war is over? For present purposes I need say no more about the importance of a site like Tepe Gawra; it ought to be evident even from our few remarks.

I have many pleasant and amusing reminiscences of the people among whom we lived and whom we employed at Tepe Gawra. The near-by village is called Fadhiliya and in 1934-35 our living quarters were situated in this village. We used to pay our men at odd intervals, for we did not want to carry the money from the bank at Mosul so regularly that highwaymen could predict the occasion and conveniently meet us en route. We would announce a paytime suddenly, whereupon there would be a great to-do. The men, of course, trusted us and did not mind if they did not have a pay day in three weeks or more; but still pay day meant lots of joyous excitement for Fadhiliya. We would arrange the money on the table, form the men into line, get out our records, and pay them off. One feature of pay day was *baksheesh*, the usual tip to men who had done their work well. One man had been taken on the staff because he was related to the mayor, a phenomenon that can happen in more than one part of the world. His work was inferior. One day when his turn came to be paid, he said, "Sahib, don't I get any *baksheesh?*" "Well," I said, "I'd love to give you some, but I don't think your work warrants it." "But," said he, "I am your nearest neighbor." "And what has that to do with it?" I asked. "Well, you see," he replied, "I live in the adjoining house; and whenever I wish, I can see all that is going on in your courtyard and I have never breathed a word of it to anyone." I gave him his *baksheesh*. I suspect he was alluding to some "shocking" scene like men and women dining at the same table or maybe even dancing together. But he gave the natives and us such a good laugh that we paid him his hush money gladly.

On another occasion Fethi, the foreman, came to me. He is one of the most intelligent men I have ever worked with. Field archaeology in "primitive" countries soon teaches one that intelligence and education do not necessarily go together. These people have the same range of intelligence as we. It is after all only an accident of birth that has placed them in Iraqian villages where people get no schooling, and that has placed us in a country where nearly everyone is literate. Fethi had got involved in a fight on account of one of his two wives. When a wife over there "walks out" on her husband, she does not go home to mother, but to father; and since this wife of Fethi had no living father, she went home to brother. Brother happened to be our day watchman, who guarded the excavation on Sundays, holidays, and when it rained; an easy and coveted job fetching double pay. After his sister came to him complaining of Fethi, her husband, the two men got into a brawl, after which the brother went off to the mound to take up his post as watchman. Fethi came to me and said, "Sahib, I have always served you faithfully, and I am willing to do anything in the world for you. Now I have one favor to ask, the first I have ever asked of you: Please fire my brother-in-law." "Indeed, I should like to oblige you," I said, "for I am not exactly fond of him myself. But we Frankish men [they have been calling occidentals "Franks" since the Crusades] have a code whereby we act without prejudice. So unless your brother-in-law is remiss in his duties, I cannot discharge him. But I will do this for you: Let us take the automobile and drive out to the mound and see whether your brother-in-law is perchance negligent." We did so and then as we walked up the mound, we heard the brother-in-law snoring, for he had been exhausted by the fight. I went up and shook him awake, and said, "We are not paying you for sleeping here. Thieves might have come and stolen all our equipment while you slept. You are fired." As his hapless brother-in-law walked off the mound, Fethi, with a beatific look, raised his eyes and hands toward heaven and in gratitude and adoration cried out: "Allah is a good God!"

A mufettish or government inspector was assigned to our excavation. He was a "gentleman of the old school," in his middle fifties, who had left his wife and two grown-up sons in Baghdad for the winter. So here he was, a grass widower, spending all his money on liquor in Mosul, the big city, which is just as wicked today as was its predecessor Nineveh in antiquity. The villagers distrust their city brethren and dislike their "godless" ways. Villagers are mostly good Moslems and disapprove of winebibbing, which is only permitted to the faithful in Paradise. The mufettish never could save any money and yet he greatly admired several of the local marriage-able girls (which means those from 12 to 15 years old in the East) and wanted to marry at least one of them. The difficulty was that none of the fathers would marry off a daughter on credit; so our inspector was a very unhappy man.

Another site in the neighborhood was Tell Billa. It was unfortunately owned by many different people and it was therefore difficult to buy or rent any considerable area for excavation. One section owned by the church in a neighboring town could be bought outright, which we did. Accordingly we did not have to spend our time filling it in afterwards to render it ready for cultivation again. Other areas had to be acquired from less agree-able owners.

Much of the soil just below the surface was honeycombed with tombs of Persian periods and underneath that we found a level datable to the Achaemenian period, which period was terminated by Alexander the Great. However, the Achaemenian level was not found throughout the mound. Tell Billa is unusually large, and the stratification is not uniform in all parts. The situation is quite different at Tepe Gawra, where all of the limited space was utilized in all the strata.

The Achaemenian occupation followed two Assyrian settlements, one in the ninth, the other in the thirteenth century B.C., corresponding to two distinct strata. In the earlier we chanced upon clay tablets; this discovery is the more important because texts of this Middle Assyrian period are relatively rare. Among other things they gave the name of Tell Billa as Shibaniba, a city long known from cuneiform inscriptions. One of the city gates of Nineveh is named after Shibaniba.

The third level was Hurrian, corresponding in time and in culture to the first three levels of Tepe Gawra. One of the objects found at this Hurrian level was a model votive shrine, made of little bricks with a different figure incised on many of the bricks. It had collapsed, but was restored from the position in which the bricks were found.

A seal cylinder seemingly found in the Hurrian level taught us a valuable lesson. At the time of discovery (1931) we thought that since it had been found at that level it was accordingly to be dated in the second millennium B.C., or slightly before. Now, however, it turns out to belong to the period of Uruk in the fourth millen-

At work on Tepe Gawra: removing Level VIII so as to reach the earlier town below it.

Unearthing the buried cities at Tell Beit Mirsim. As this picture and the one above illustrate, limestone is the prevalent building material in Palestine as against brick in Mesopotamia.

The Iraqi machine-gun squad that kept the peace in Bashiqa during Ramadan.

From left to right: a Yezidi, the author, and an oriental Christian, in the mountains of Kurdistan.

nium B.C. This is certain from stratified remains in Babylonia. Thus it turned out to be an ancient seal preserved as an heirloom for perhaps about two thousand years before it was apparently buried in Level III! The phenomenon of heirlooms should never be lost sight of in the case of durable, precious objects, for such things may be handed down from generation to generation even for thousands of years—witness our museums today. All things being equal, when a stratum is destroyed or abandoned, nothing in that stratum is later than the time of the destruction that buried the stratum, though there is no limit to how much *earlier* certain objects may be. Most of the objects are roughly contemporary with their architectural surroundings; heirlooms are older.

Level V at Tell Billa corresponded to Level VI at Tepe Gawra, and below that there were several prehistoric levels; but Tell Billa as a whole is not to be compared with Tepe Gawra as a site going back deep into the past.

The most dangerous crisis I ever experienced in the course of all my expeditions took place at Tell Billa in December, 1932, and January, 1933. The Moslem fast of Ramadan fell at that time, and the religious problem became acute, as it always does during Ramadan. Most of the natives in our village were Yezidis or "Devil-worshipers," whose religion is calculated to propitiate Satan. They hold that since God is all-good, He is incapable of any evil, and therefore requires no prayer. God is therefore to be loved but not worshiped. Satan, however, being purely bad, must be constantly appeased. This appeasement policy is hardly so Satanic as the recent European variety, and none of us archaeologists found anything objectionable in these Devil-worshipers, in our dealings with them. However, their Moslem neighbors do not feel the same way. To be sure, Moslems and Yezidis usually get along well enough except during Ramadan when the Moslems, irritated by their arduous fasting, become pugnacious. Theology tends to become very dogmatic on an empty stomach. We therefore used to separate our workmen in Ramadan according to faith: Moslems in one area, Christians and Devil-worshipers in another. One day in December I was conducting the work at Tell Billa when I heard shots, and soon a couple of horsemen came galloping down from the near-by hills announcing that two Yezidis had been killed by Kurdish Moslems. Not being fully initiated into the institutions of the land, I expected open war to follow. My foreman, however, allayed my fears by informing me that two killings at this time of year were routine matters. One year the Yezidis kill two Kurdish Moslems, while the next year the Kurdish Moslems kill two Yezidis. Therefore there would be no more killings for another year; at least not from this particular feud. But the following day some Yezidis looted some Moslem shops in order to express their resentment. So the next day the Moslems showed their indignation by breaking into a Yezidi shrine and destroying a door and some of the cult objects. On the third day, we found the Qoran from the Mosque torn and strewn upon a dung heap. At this point we decided to suspend the excavations, for there was no telling what might happen next. Anyway the laborers themselves wanted to be on hand to defend their homes if necessary. A couple of nights later, at about three in the morning, our butler came to my bedside and with many apologies for disturbing me, reported that Kurdish tribesmen were gathering on Jebel Bashiqa, the ridge just above our village, and were apparently going to strike at dawn. They were almost certain to loot our quarters for the gold and precious objects that we had found or, what was more in the way of truth, the valuable objects they imagined we had found. For the town it meant fire and the sword. I rubbed my eyes and we held a "council of war." We decided to pick two expert riders and mount them on black horses so that they would not readily be seen in the dark, and send them by different roads to Mosul in the hope that one at least would get through in time to bring military aid from Mosul. Meanwhile, we stood on the roof to see developments. There was just one thing I did resent about the situation, and that was to see the encampment of Bedouin not far from our house just outside the village, sitting calmly on their haunches waiting to share in the loot as soon as the Kurds came down to attack us. I felt it was not a neighborly way of acting. But the chief instinct of the Bedouin is to loot when the looting is good, and you have to pardon him for it as you forgive a cat for killing mice.

I do not want to dramatize the situation; nor can I see any reason either to exaggerate or underestimate the danger we were in. The fact is that an hour before the

Kurds were to strike, an R.A.F. plane came flying low over the village, striking terror into the hearts of the Kurdish tribesmen, who have a great respect for army planes, especially when they fly low. Half an hour later armored cars—another modern machine, the purpose of which the Kurdish tribesman thoroughly understands— occupied the town till the end of Ramadan, and even a while after, to keep the peace. Neither that year nor on subsequent campaigns did we have any trouble or need of protection. In passing, let me say we had many reasons to be grateful to the R.A.F.; for taking aerial photographs for us, and on that occasion for protecting us from pillaging and fire, and for other kindnesses too numerous to mention.

The stratigraphic method may also be illustrated from the excavations at Tell Beit Mirsim. We had to rent the land there, and there was no end to the negotiations and discussions and quibbling that went on beforehand. The tell is owned by a whole clan, and to rent even an acre of agriculturally inferior land might require the consent of fifty to a hundred stubborn Arabs. Yet such transactions had to be done before we could begin to dig.

Tell Beit Mirsim has at least nine distinct levels, each terminated by violent destruction, so that all are sharply distinguishable from the levels below and above. The earliest destruction happened about 2300 B.C.; the latest probably in 588 B.C. when Nebuchadnezzar devastated Judah. The lowest level, designated as J, was quite fragmentary, its only remains being potsherds found in crevices and caves in the bedrock. Level H (the letter I is omitted lest it be confused with the Roman numeral) probably had a town wall as indicated by a massive structure built under another immediately above it. G and F were culturally almost indistinguishable though stratigraphically quite distinct. F had re-used the town wall of G, widening and strengthening it. E and D belonged to the Hyksos period (the eighteenth and seventeenth centuries). This was the first time this period could be divided on stratigraphic evidence into an earlier and a later subdivision, thus enabling us to refine our knowledge of the culture of the Hyksos age. For instance, in E a house was built with a line of three wooden columns, on stone bases, upholding the roof of the main room. The house was re-used in the next period, but the columns were removed, the bases covered, and an open-court type of house displaced the old colonnaded house whose chief room had been roofed.

A good many small objects were found in all these levels. For instance, in the Hyksos level· we found a figure of a goddess with a serpent entwined around her. We discovered gaming pieces, showing how the people amused themselves. We unearthed various kinds of art objects, including quite good figures of animals incised on bone.

In Level C there were two phases separated by destruction debris. In the earlier phase there were certain Mycenean sherds that were not found in the upper level, but most of the ceramic types were common to both phases.

B and A were Israelite levels, marked by quite a few

destructions. One was doubtless the destruction by Sennacherib, who devastated Judah in 701. The town was never rebuilt after the destruction dealt by Nebuchadnezzar in 588 B.C.

For the latest Israelite city we had a complete layout in the excavated area, including the city wall, fortifications, city gates, private dwellings, and even industrial establishments such as wine presses (which have now disappeared from the land, since good Moslems do not make or consume alcoholic drinks). The chief industry, however, had apparently been the weaving and dyeing of wool, for we found many loom weights, spindle whorls and dye vats. From the standpoint of religion, it was interesting to find that the Israelite houses had many Astarte figurines proving that the Hebrew common people in their popular religion gave their prophets good reason for complaining. Officially, as we shall see in a later chapter, the Judeans were worshiping Yahweh, and not the goddess of fertility. The fact that our churches do not sanction astrology, fortunetelling, and other superstitions does not prevent an astonishing number of our fellow citizens from subscribing to astrological journals or from resorting to palmists, crystal gazers and spiritualists, in plain defiance of Scripture. Similarly, the Judeans, though officially worshipers of Yahweh and Yahweh alone, made a place for the popular, unsanctioned practices of the times, and so we uncover their Astarte figurines connected with the fertility cult.

Among the objects discovered was a stone censer, from about 700 B.C., the best of its interesting type found so far. We found one piece of it early in the season, another a couple of weeks later in another part of the mound. The two parts dovetailed and formed a single piece. The bowl of the censer was carved in the shape of a lion's head. The priest apparently blew on the incense through the stem leading to the bowl. The construction was essentially the same as the modern smoking pipe.

The destruction of the city in 588 B.C. was so dreadful that adobe was burned to a bright red while limestone was slivered and even pulverized. After many centuries the burned stone combined with the annual rains to form a lime incrustation on the pottery and other objects, witnessing the intensity of Tell Beit Mirsim's last destruction.

The people now living about Tell Beit Mirsim show an interesting variety of cultures, existing side by side. Our laborers still live in the near-by caves during the summer months. Other tribes wander about pitching their tents; and still others live in village houses. It is a wonderful human experience to be an archaeologist in the Near East; if for no other reason than to get a sense of perspective and to realize that there are states of culture besides our own, and that our ways of living are not the only ones. Field archaeology simultaneously teaches us about mankind in time and place.

Before leaving the subject of Tell Beit Mirsim, I should like to tell some of my experiences among the troglodyte Arabs there. As I confessed in the first chapter, I often allowed myself to be inveigled into the practice of quack medicine. At Tell Beit Mirsim I conducted an out-of-door clinic where I treated scores of patients daily. Eye infections are particularly rife and often lead to blindness in one or both eyes. By administering a 5 per cent solution of argyrol I was able to clear up many cases of conjunctivitis within ten days or two weeks. A father with several children came to the "clinic" so that I might treat those of the children who had eye infections. To clean up the children for the "doctor," he wiped the eyes of the infected children with a corner of his robe and then, for good measure, wiped the eyes of the healthy children with the same corner. There was no point in telling him about germs. Instead I remarked that pus was full of tiny jinn that caused eye disease. This intelligible doctrine was spread throughout the community with good results.

For a while I was dispensing castor oil for those who needed a laxative. However, Arabs are so fond of the flavor of castor oil that great multitudes began to clamor daily for a dose of what they call *esh shorba* "the drink (par excellence)," rather than *zeit el khirwa*, which is the correct word for "castor oil." I determined that something radical had to be done when I detected men getting back into line for a second dose. To my relief, I discovered that Arabs abhor epsom salts, which accordingly was substituted for castor oil in my *materia medica*.

I had a supply of iodine for applying to the slight wounds that are inevitable in the course of manual work. Soon I discovered that the men were fond of having iodine on them. The reason seems to be its resemblance to henna which they put on their finger nails and else-where, as well as on the bodies of their sheep, for ward-ing off misfortune and disease. However, I did not realize how much they prized iodine, until one day an Arab asked to have some of it put on him. I asked him where the wound was. When he told me he had no wound and I informed him that only injured men were entitled to iodine, he walked away and returned in a few minutes with a generous gash in his hand. He there-upon got his iodine plus a sermon on folly.

By doctoring the natives I learned of all sorts of curious folkways. For example, a Bedouin boy came to me to see what I could do for his ankle, which had a hemispherical chunk neatly burned out of it. Upon in-quiring how on earth he had got such a burn, he told me he had been greatly fatigued by a round-trip to far-off Jerusalem on foot. Upon returning he resorted to this old Bedouin cure for acute weariness: He placed some tinder on his ankle and set a live coal on the tin-der. The coal burned through the tinder and into his flesh, whereupon all his fatigue disappeared and new life entered his weary frame. Luckily the burn was fresh and uninfected. I kept it dressed clean, and by the end of the summer his ankle was safely healed though of course permanently scarred.

My favorite laborer at Tell Beit Mirsim was a power-ful fellow named Isa. His strength earned him the post of rockcrusher. When the men would come upon rocks too large to move, Isa would crack the rocks with a sledge-hammer. During an earlier campaign at Tell Beit

Mirsim, Isa had tried to intimidate the men into paying him part of their wages for "protection." To establish his authority, he banded them together and demanded a general increase in pay, shouting: "I am sheikh over all these men!" Dr. Albright, refusing to recognize Isa's claims, retorted: "You are not a full-fledged sheikh but merely a half[-baked] sheikh." Whereupon the men laughed and deserted Isa. Isa walked away in shame but sometime later apologized and was reinstated. He never again misbehaved. He told me that cave life in the summer was quite to his liking but he did not fancy spending the winter with the clan. Instead he committed a minor crime, such as stealing a camel, late every fall and thus managed to be jailed. Isa was strongly pro-British. He related how terrible conditions were under the Turks, when jails were lice-ridden and cold, in which edible food was only obtainable by wealthy inmates whose servants brought them dainties from home. "But the English," said Isa, beaming like a grateful child, "have made jail a pleasure. The cells are clean, the food is fine, and the prisoners get meat several times a week. Each of us has two changes of clothes, one of which is always freshly washed. Instead of confining us to our cells, the English see that we get enough fresh air and exercise. Ah, Khwajah, the English rule well and I look forward to another pleasant winter in their prisons."

Another of the many notable characters at Tell Beit Mirsim was our night watchman, who had earned the coveted title of Hajji ("Pilgrim") because he had made the sacred pilgrimage to Mecca. It amused us to hear how

Hajji had attained the respected rank of "Pilgrim." During the first World War, the Turks came to the district in search of men for the cavalry. Hajji was conscripted and his company was forced to go to Mecca on a military assignment. Thus may a man have sanctity thrust upon him!

CHAPTER V

GRAVES AND OTHER "INTRUSIONS"

DESPITE A word of warning in the discussion of stratigraphic excavation, we have perhaps given the impression that excavation consists of merely uncovering stratum after stratum, like taking layers off a layer cake. It is, of course, not so simple as all that, for a mound, having been constructed largely by the accidents of history, cannot be expected to consist of neat, even layers one on top of another. In the science of stratigraphy one must use great caution, for sometimes an object of a much later period may be found in an earlier level. One common reason for such mishaps is the fact that certain animals, especially moles, may dig holes from the top of a mound through several earlier levels, so that coins or small objects may fall through to plague the excavator who encounters them in a lower stratum. In addition to falling, objects may even rise above their level. Potsherds in loose soil tend to wriggle their way upward, particularly after heavy rains, so that at times such objects intrude at a *higher* level than that to which they properly belong. The rule we must always bear in mind is that "one swallow does not make a summer," and that the fact that an isolated object is found at a certain level means little or nothing by itself. Inferences from individual objects must be made with the greatest caution, and only when many facts corroborate one another, can we be justified in drawing broad conclusions from their context.

In one sense intrusions are inevitable. For while stratigraphic excavation consists essentially of digging down to the floor level and clearing all the structures on a given floor or street, this is obviously not the whole story. A moment's reflection would tell us that the foundations of every structure are always below the floor level, to say nothing of such things as pipes installed beneath the pavement to carry off sewage. So quite a few features of a city are necessarily below street level. Indeed, a good catch question to stump a beginner in archaeology is: To what stratum may an object belong if it is found five inches below the floor? The answer is, of course, that it need not belong to the level below the floor but instead to the one above, since the foundations must have been dug at least five inches below street level.

In order to understand the problem of the archaeologist, one must also comprehend the mode of life of the ancient inhabitants. In those blessed days before the invention of aerial warfare, a town wall was ordinarily enough to keep enemies out. Indeed a "town" or "city" (as distinguished from a "village") was a settlement surrounded by a wall. It was not necessarily a great center of population and thus some "villages" were larger than certain "towns." The "town" being protected by a surrounding wall afforded a haven for the inhabitants from the neighboring villages in times of siege. During such crises there would inevitably be a heavy concentration of people within the walls, and in order to withstand a siege successfully the inhabitants would have to have an adequate supply of water and food. Under such conditions surface space within the town would obviously be at a premium, so that water and food would have to be stored in underground cisterns and pits. For this reason, every ancient town I know of in the Near East has cisterns for holding water, and grain pits for storing food, sunk down into earlier strata. These storage pits and cisterns constitute the most extensive type of intrusion that confronts the excavator, and while they extend down through earlier towns, they belong to the upper level from which they were dug. When one speaks of stratigraphic excavation, therefore, one does not mean stratigraphy in the strict sense of what a leveling machine might tell us, but rather excavation of the complete settlement occupied at a given time. In other words, if you are digging a town of 2000 B.C. and encounter a cistern or pit intruding into earlier levels, that intrusion must be cleared at the same time, for what you are endeavoring to do is to clear the complete habitation of a particular period, and a leveling machine would be quite misleading under those circumstances.

But how does the excavator realize that he has come across an intrusion into an earlier level? There are numerous criteria that show him this: For one thing, a discoloration of the soil often indicates a structure which is not the same as those round about. The archaeologist will then have to instruct the laborers to dig straight down till they reach the bottom of the intrusion. There are also other criteria, for store pits and cisterns tend also to have a lining of plaster or stone to keep them waterproof or to enable them to preserve organic matter.

Even intrusions, however, are subject to certain stratigraphic rules. For example, an intrusive structure must antedate the nearest unbroken floor level lying directly above it. Accordingly, the excavator must pay strict attention to the state of even the most unimpressive-looking floors so as to record their bearing on possible, but unforeseen, intrusions below. For once a floor is removed, the archaeologist has only his records as evidence.

To take an example of a major intrusion: At the eighth city at Tepe Gawra (counting from the top), dating from the fourth millennium B.C., we came across a huge pit. It so happened that it went down twenty meters (over 65 feet) through not less than twelve earlier cities (and in all probability there were more than twelve) into the virgin soil beneath the mound. Obviously, the law of gravity has it that anything dropped into space will fall until something solid stops it; therefore the excavator is not going to find much till he gets near the bottom of a pit. That particular pit at Gawra was a cistern used for storing water. Since the objects dropped into it in antiquity had fallen to the bottom, we had to dig through nearly twenty meters of hard debris before the objects that had been dropped into it began to be found. This means that such work is dull for a long time; and, I may add, dangerous for the laborers unless careful precautions are taken. The usual method is to erect a tripod or some other sort of structure over the pit so that buckets may be raised and lowered on wheels or pulleys. Thus the soil is removed and the bottom is reached, where the interesting objects lie. We pay the men more than the usual wages for such arduous, routine work, and every precaution is taken to insure safety, for if anything were dropped from twenty meters above, a person below might be critically injured. The pottery and other objects found at the bottom of the cistern belonged not to the level flush with the bottom but to the point where they were originally made and used and from which they had been dropped.

This brings up another problem that we have not yet considered: the problem of dumping. When the ancients constructed that pit and dug through not less than twelve earlier cities, they threw the debris over the side of the mound as they cleared the pit. Assuming for the sake of simplicity that they did all their dumping in one spot, that would mean that what came latest would be on the bottom while the deeper (and therefore earlier) debris would be on top; so that their artificial mound of debris would have the exact reverse of the chronology of the natural mound: in the mound, the earliest would be lowest, but where the dumping was done the latest would be lowest. And incidentally, not only the ancients did that, but we archaeologists do it all the time. One

must therefore beware of applying the rules of stratigraphic excavation uncritically.

Intrusions unfortunately tend to play havoc with the
architecture below. This pit at Tepe Gawra damaged
buildings of at least twelve cities beneath so that the
architect is not usually gladdened by such intrusions. For
example, in the third city at Tell Beit Mirsim a great
part of Level C was seriously damaged by cisterns and
grain pits sunk from the Israelite levels.

The most widely publicized type of intrusion is the
grave. However, a burial ground or necropolis need not
be intrusive. Thus the cemeteries of the average modern
American city involve no intrusion into earlier cultural
levels. Nor is there any cultural intrusion in rock tombs
like those in the famous Valley of the Kings, in Egypt.
Such Egyptian tombs are geological but not archaeological intrusions and therefore do not concern us.

When we have to do with unknown or little-known
cultures, it is especially desirable to excavate stratified
towns before the necropolises associated with them. In
digging stratified cities the archaeologist gets a chronological sequence for the cultural relics unearthed, but he
is far less certain of the chronological order of graves.
But since funerary objects are for the most part objects
of daily life, we can date them from the stratified towns
with which they are associated. Such funerary objects
commonly include vessels for holding food or drink;
finery, jewelry, perfume, and toilet articles; musical in-
struments and so forth. At Tepe Gawra there was one
pathetic little grave with the skeleton of a child holding

a clay flute in his tiny hand. The future life was essentially a replica of life on earth, and therefore unrobbed graves tend to be filled with objects of daily life.

To take a few specific illustrations of graves: At Tell Billa in northern Assyria, as we have noted, the top part of the mound was filled with those intrusive burials, mostly of Achaemenian and later Persian periods. Some of the graves are known as capsule burials in which the head and chest of the skeleton are laid in one large pottery jar, and the legs in another. Some of these capsule graves lay only a few inches under the modern surface of the mound. There are many other types of burial, classified according to structure. Some burials have special structures associated with them: actual mausoleums or sepulchers or tomb-structures in which the dead are laid. Sometimes people would dig down and appropriate an earlier building; or a part of it, merely supplementing it with the necessary walls to complete a burial structure. And for that matter there are also "loose burials," where the body is simply wrapped in cloth or in a mat, laid in the soil, and covered with earth.

In the early part of 1932 I received a memorable assignment. While Sir Leonard Woolley was then conducting his last campaign at Ur he chanced to need the services of an epigraphist to read some of the Sumerian inscriptions he had found. I had the good fortune to be called to Ur from my post at Tell Billa and Tepe Gawra to do this work.

I went by car to the Great Zab River, where we had to ferry over that torrential stream to the village of

Guweir on the other side. As we reached the river the driver pointed out the very spot where an Englishman had been murdered a few days before. The whole countryside was still talking of the assassination, of which I shall have more to say presently. The "Berlin to Baghdad Railway" has not yet been built from well east of Mosul to Kirkuk, and so from out in the desert to Kirkuk the railway terminals are connected by automobile service, though the railway continues beyond Baghdad to Basra in the south. I took the train at Kirkuk, and, being an inexperienced train traveler in those parts, I had forgotten to bring blankets and found that the railroad did not supply enough for comfort during the cold night. I was touched by the generosity of some Iraqians on the train who, seeing that I was not properly equipped with bedding, contributed enough blankets to keep me warm.

In Baghdad a rather amusing experience befell me. The Director of the Iraq Museum there was then Dr. Julius Jordan. My colleagues at Tepe Gawra—whether to tease me or not I do not know—sent a telegram to be delivered to me at the Museum, but when it arrived the name of the addressee had been altered from "Gordon" to "Jordan," and delivered to the Museum director. It read, "Come back soon we miss you so," and was signed by the expedition. This naturally mystified Dr. Jordan, whose contacts with our expedition had been rather official and of not-too-intimate a character. The mystery was solved to his great relief, when I appeared on the scene.

Between the texts that I was reading for Sir Leonard Woolley at Ur, I had the thrill of watching some of the impressive royal tombs come to light. One of the burials of the later period—the period known as the Third Dynasty of Ur, towards the end of the third millennium B.C.—was a building the quality of which cannot be matched in any modern building that I have seen in Iraq. Even the present king's royal palace outside Baghdad is not to be compared with this ancient tomb of the kings of old. We sometimes make the mistake of thinking that the passage of time means progress. It would perhaps be better if we rid ourselves of the word "progress" altogether, for it hides more truth than it reveals.

But more interesting than these magnificent "Ur III" burials were the older Sumerian burials (usually without any special structure) dating back to the Early Dynastic age, from about 3000 to 2500 B.C. These graves yielded finds of exquisite beauty; such as a helmet of gold, imitating the contour of the head with a full chignon behind, with every curl wave and even the individual hairs executed superbly by the ancient craftsman. There was a golden dagger in a sheath of gold filigree which has literally never been excelled to the best of my knowledge; not even in the finest museums in Europe, where you can examine western filigree work at its best, will you find anything to eclipse the quality of workmanship of this ancient Sumerian artist. Numerous harps, to accompany the dead in their future life, were found; the metal, shell, and stone parts were still preserved; and though the wooden parts had decayed they could be restored with certainty because the harps are so faithfully depicted by contemporary artists on imperishable stone.

Those who have seen in Philadelphia, London, and Baghdad the treasures discovered at Ur know how superb these objects are. Even a cursory examination of the color plates of Sir Leonard's publication convey a rich impression of the splendor. Nor is there anything primitive about this art. The sooner we disabuse ourselves of the false idea that the primitive is equivalent to the early in point of time rather than to the low in point of quality, the better we will prepare ourselves for a truly historical attitude toward art and general culture.

I remember, as Sir Leonard took me through the tombs under excavation, how carefully we had to tread lest we crush a golden object just under the surface. If we brushed away the soil with our fingers, gold and lapis-lazuli and carnelian would peer forth from the earth. It was fantastic to see such splendor coming from the ground. Even an archaeologist is not used to that kind of thing! It was one find in a thousand.

The burials there were so numerous that Sir Leonard had excavated 1,850 of them in a rather limited area, and those represented but a half or perhaps only a third of what had been there, for many others had been wholly or partly obliterated.

The method that Sir Leonard Woolley used to reconstruct a chronology of the burials is known as the "group method." He would not reckon with graves unless there were at least five superimposed one on the other. And at that, only if the relationship of the five (or more) was such that none of the graves had been intruded upon in order to make room for another, would he use the grave group for establishing a chronology (paying strict attention to the objects found in each grave). Properly assuming that the lower was the earlier burial and by combining groups which overlapped in time, he skillfully attempted to establish a chronology based on stratigraphic evidence.

This is the opposite of the method devised by Sir Flinders Petrie, who, in the absence of sufficient stratigraphy established sequence dates according to stylistic features of the finds. Thus he took as a criterion the "wavy-ledge" handles on pottery vessels of the Early Bronze Age in Egypt and found that this handle got smaller and smaller until it became vestigal and eventually disappeared. The difficulty here was that without a starting or stopping point you could not tell which way the development proceeds. To use the language of biology: Without being able to fix one end of the development, Sir Flinders could not be sure whether the tiny wavy-ledge handle was rudimentary (i.e., the beginning of the development) or vestigial (i.e., the end of the development). Luckily, Sir Flinders found the necessary bit of stratigraphic evidence to show it was vestigial. Essentially, then, Sir Flinders' sequence dating was stylistic, Sir Leonard's group method, stratigraphic.

Sir Leonard used an interesting system of rewarding his laborers. Paying *baksheesh* to the men is a very important thing, for if they are not rewarded for valuable finds they may begin to steal. What he did was to divide his laborers into groups of one pick man, one shovel man, and a few basket boys; and each group was to share the rewards collectively. He placed enemies rather than friends together in these groups and since the whole group had to share the reward, one could try to steal from the others only at the risk of his head; the others would not put up with it. So by means of the very strong human factor of animosity, Sir Leonard managed, I think, to have very little stolen from him.

He found so much gold that it was impossible to reward the men fully according to its gold value. Sir Flinders Petrie has told me that he always weighs the gold and pays according to its sterling value, so that there would be no point in the men's stealing antiquities and going elsewhere to sell them. Sir Flinders happens to have found more gold at Tell el Ajjul (south of Gaza) than anyone else anywhere in Palestine, a fact which he attributes exclusively to this system of rewarding, gold for gold. I think that the method is indeed very effective, and might well be imitated by others wherever it is practicable; but I believe that there is also an element of luck in the finding of so much gold by one man.

I might say here that the Oriental is to be trusted more than many of us might imagine. He has a great sense of honor. In 1927, on the closing day of that year's campaign at Ur, that now famous filigree dagger was found. It is of course priceless for its historical and artistic value, but even its monetary worth was obvious to every Arab on the site. Sir Leonard took the sheikh aside and addressed him something like this: "You see that this excavation is not yet complete. We hope to return to it next year. You know and I know that it is full of gold. I will show you how full it is." Here he scraped away a little of the soil and several gold beads fell out. Sir Leonard knew that the tribe would be on its honor to keep that site intact for him, but he did put secret markings here and there so that later he could check whether it had been disturbed. When he came back the following year, nothing had been touched. Such are the standards of tribal honor among the Arabs. They feel that if they betray a trust they are unworthy to go on living. You can therefore appeal to their honor with complete confidence. I have never personally experienced a single case of a breach of honor among the Arabs.

At this point I wish to make a comment of appreciation of Sir Leonard's work. His field technique is superb. But apart from that, the finds that he has made at Ur are even more important than the rich finds made at the tomb of King Tutankhamen by Carter and Carnarvon. The latter discoveries, however splendid, did not add much to our knowledge of history or even of art, whereas what Sir Leonard Woolley found at Ur opened up a great and new chapter in the history of art, going back to that remarkable people, the Sumerians, of whom we are still learning much as the years go by and to whom even occidental civilization is indebted.

On my way back to Tepe Gawra and Tell Billa I had the pleasure of sharing a compartment in the train with M. André Parrot, a distinguished though young French archaeologist who has since made spectacular discoveries at Mari on the Euphrates. I had not yet been in France, and my knowledge of the French language was then limited to reading. M. Parrot knew not a word of English. So we conversed for over ten hours in Arabic together—a remarkable linguistic experience for a Frenchman and an American.

I drove back from Baghdad to Mosul in a car with several Arab gentlemen and an Arab driver, and as we passed the ancient town of Erbil (the site of one of Alexander's great victories), our car began to show signs of motor trouble. We got to the town of Guweir before sundown, but the police officials there would not allow us to proceed across the Great Zab. That Englishman had been killed only a few weeks before, and the government was taking no chances with travelers. In vain did we ask the chief of police for special permission to cross the river. While our car was parked before the police station in the little mud-brick village, a sack of oranges that one of my fellow travelers was bringing to Mosul as a gift was stolen from the car. One of our party went up to the chief of police, pounded his fist on the table, and said, "It may interest you to know that I am a relative of the governor. Unless we see those oranges in the next five minutes, there will be a new chief of police here." And within a few minutes the oranges were found and returned. I have never been able to determine whether the police of that village were supersleuths or just plain thieves.

We realized that we would have to spend the night there, and ordered supper and lodging at the "tea house," which is not what its name might convey to Western ears. In that part of the world a tea house, far from being a place for ladies and occasionally their escorts, is a place where the good-for-nothings gather to waste time, to gamble and do various things that may include the plotting of a theft or even a murder or two. That tea house was full of sinister-looking men, with knives in their belts, muttering in their beards as they gambled and sipped their coffee and tea. But we had our supper, and very good it was with broth, chicken, rice, olives, Arab bread, and the like. We all ate in brotherly Eastern fashion, with our fingers, out of a common dish. We had no knives or forks but only spoons for the soup which we drank from a single bowl set before our party. After we had beguiled a part of the night in exchanging stories, we decided to go to sleep and stretched ourselves along the wall, letting the habitués enjoy themselves till morning if they wished. I lay with my head in one corner of the room while a young Arab of our party lay along the adjoining wall with his head toward the same corner. While the others slept he poured a tale of woe into my ears. He was, he said, a Christian, and therefore, unlike the Moslems, was allowed to see his fiancée's face before marriage. He had got two days' leave from his job in Baghdad to see her in Mosul, and at best he would have had less than one day with his beloved; but now, with this delay, he might not even have time to see her at all, or at most, which would be almost worse, he could see her only for a moment to say hello and farewell. He went off into a poetic tirade the like of which I had never heard. Only an Oriental could have uttered it. "Do you think I am flesh and blood, my friend?" he queried. "If you do, you are wrong; I am stone. Here is my dagger; plunge it into my breast and you will see that no blood will flow." And so on, and so on, till I finally fell asleep. For all I know, he soliloquized all night.

For breakfast next morning we had native bread and tea and a pleasant mixture of honey and camel cream. And the bill for supper, lodging, and breakfast came to something under fifteen cents apiece.

Next morning I was back at Tell Billa and Tepe Gawra with my neighbors the Devil-worshipers. I had returned from the glamorous tombs of Ur to the less spectacular but no less interesting and even earlier graves at Tepe Gawra. I was to spend three winter campaigns at Gawra. It was during the last of these that I was walking one morning to the mound with our government inspector, the mufettish whom I have already mentioned. That day he was telling me that it was very generous of us to give him the same food that we ourselves ate (we sent trays out to him regularly), "But," he said, "I am not used to your sauces and your pies and your cakes and those delicacies of Paris and London and New York." He picked up a handful of soil and let it run through his fingers. "Do you see this dirt?" he asked. "Well, this is whence I come. I am a son of this soil. And I don't want the cakes and pies of the capitals of the Occident. Just let me have some nuts and raisins and cheese and onions, for I can no longer bear your fancy fare." I told him I would take his plea to Mr. Charles Bache, the director, which I did. From then on the inspector got native food and everyone was happy.

When we got to the mound the inspector did as he always did, and as government officials are said to do in many other parts of the world, he fell asleep immediately; and his snores could be heard from one end of the mound to the other. But, also, as usual, he had made me promise to wake him up if anything interesting took place, and so I always did. This day it was not long before I had reason to wake him up, for we found an interesting infant burial, with a tiny skeleton curled up in an open bowl. At Gawra of the fourth millennium, infant burials were found under many buildings. At first we were inclined to think that this was religious infanticide, such as the familiar slaying of the first-born in order to give to the god the first fruit of the womb as well as of the soil. This would be very interesting, and it is a possibility. But the frequency of infant burials was more likely due to the generally high infant mortality which has always characterized those parts of the world and which is taken for granted rather than viewed with alarm. The simple explanation is usually the better one. For while a religious or mystical explanation may be more attractive, the simple one is apt to be closer to the truth. When we chanced upon that infant burial, I woke the inspector, who came and looked intently at the little grave as it came to light under the nimble fingers of our laborers. I could see that he was deeply moved. He grew tenser and tenser and finally he went off into an oration that one could only expect from an Oriental. He burst forth, "O babe, lucky art thou who hast died before thy time! Lucky art thou, who hast passed from this wicked world without seeing its misery and suffering. Lucky art thou who hast not beheld what we now see: the nations of Europe and Asia with swords and daggers drawn, about to hack one another to bits." This was in 1935, four and a half years before the outbreak of the present war; and so you can see that even a lowly government inspector given to sleeping on the job might have some insight into the impending future of mankind.

Many of the Gawra skeletons were found in appropriated or partly appropriated structures of earlier levels. Some of the graves were unrifled and yielded numerous objects of gold, electrum, and semi-precious stone. Notable is a hair ornament of ivory with four bands of gold and rows of semiprecious stones in three different colors. Several ivory combs identical in shape with present-day pocket combs witnessed the truth of Ecclesiastes, who has pointed out for the ages that nothing is new under the sun.

The qualifications of the natives we employed in excavating graves are worthy of further mention. This task calls for delicate work, if the bones are not to be disturbed; or if the discoloration of the soil, which is usually all that is left of the mats the dead were wrapped in, is not to be destroyed beyond recognition. Those who work on graves are specialists, with a delicacy of touch that would be hard to improve on in any part of the world. Of course, they still need constant supervision, for you cannot leave even the best laborer on his own, no matter how loyal or intelligent or careful he may be. The excavator must always watch or assist the natives at their work, and as they uncover the grave by degrees, he must be there to take pictures or make sketches and field notes in order to record the exact position of the body, its orientation, and all sorts of details whether or not he has any explanation for them at the time. There may arise the necessity of preserving some of the antiquities on the spot. The application of paraffin or some other substance may be indicated before a delicate antiquity is removed. Sometimes, too, skulls and other bones must be removed in some such special way so that they may later be examined by a physical anthropologist. When anything of interest or value is found, the laborer who discovered it is to get the reward, provided of course he did not damage it in the finding. As a rule the native specialist who clears the grave is not the one who first discovered it. That specialist receives higher pay for his skill, while the discoverer gets a reward for his luck, and observation and carefulness. Before leaving the subject of *baksheesh*, let us note that while the archaeologist must forestall theft by giving a fair reward, he must also be on his guard against "salting"; for in order to get *baksheesh*, laborers sometimes bring an antiquity from outside and say they found it in the excavation. Usually it is easy to catch the culprit.

For instance, one day a laborer handed me a corroded Turkish coin which he said he had just unearthed. Since he was digging fourth millennium soil without any intrusions from a later period, I fired him immediately. I did not explain why a nineteenth century A.D. coin could not have come out of Level IX at Tepe Gawra. As far as the natives were concerned, I could detect their falsehoods by magic and so they did not try to "salt" anything else on us that year, as far as I know.

One of the Gawra graves contained two bodies arranged in their original symmetrical position—face to face, and knee to knee. They probably died, and so were buried, at the same time. It is possible, of course, that the husband died and the wife was killed to accompany him into the next world but again we have no proof of this, nor do we know whether this custom, known in other parts of the world, prevailed here; for this was the only example we found of this type of burial, and it is gratuitous to build up a theory on an isolated fact.

In excavating graves such as those at Ur, where the excavator constantly finds interesting objects, where he can brush aside the soil and find red and yellow gold peering up at him from the earth, the greatness of the thrill imposes added restraint upon him. For in this kind of work one must constantly curb his impulse to hurry from one discovery to another. One must exercise the greatest self-control, for such work must be done slowly if the evidence is to be preserved. The difference between the object found by an illicit dealer or by a thief and sold in the open market to a private collector or museum, and the object found by an excavator digging with scientific accuracy, is that the latter is associated with a context while the former is not. For historical purposes there is all the difference in the world.

Mr. William Gad, surveying the walls of Level A at
Tell Beit Mirsim, assisted by two local boys.

An infant burial at Tepe Gawra.

A double burial at Tepe Gawra. A hand of the skeleton on the left is in its mouth. The white material visible between the skeletons is what was left of the mat on which they were laid.

CHAPTER VI

GLYPTIC ART

ART, IN the broad sense of the sum total of man's handicraft, may be divided for practical purposes into two categories: (1) architectural and (2) movable units. The former category includes fortifications, temples, private dwellings, streets, tombs, cisterns, and other structures. The latter category is even more general, for it embraces a host of things ranging from needles to colossal statues. (Inscriptions are of such a specialized nature that they are treated in a class by themselves; and four full chapters will be devoted to them.) The movable units are best divided into (a) fine art and (b) artifacts. A product of fine art is usually made with primary regard for aesthetic quality and may or may not have a utilitarian purpose. We shall use "artifact" in the sense of a movable man-made object exclusive of fine art. With artifacts, utility is regularly of primary consideration, aesthetic appeal being secondary or even absent. Utensils, weapons, tools, furniture, and the like are generally artifacts. Jewelry, sculpture, paintings, and the like are normally fine art.

In the ancient Near East, as we have noted, pottery is the most common, and archaeologically the most valuable, art object. In pre-Hellenistic Palestine, where there is a relative dearth of inscriptions and fine art, the study of ceramics has been refined to a remarkable degree. However, Mesopotamia and Egypt yield so much fine art and writing that archaeologists in those lands tend to pay less attention to the ceramics of well-attested ages except when the pottery under consideration is fine art.

Seals are more revealing and are intrinsically more interesting than pottery, or for that matter, than any other class of art in ancient Western Asia. Indeed their interest and the durability of the stone from which they are usually made, explain the stratigraphic drawback of seals: their persistence as heirlooms. However, a non-intrusive seal is never later than its archaeologic context, and so if the scholar is critical, he may use seals to good advantage.

Seals, of the stamp type, were in use as early as the fifth millennium. Their invention resulted essentially from the possessive instinct of mankind (though seals were often used as phylacteries too). Thus, to show that a jar of wine or grain belonged to him, a man would cover the stopper of the jar with clay and impress his seal while the clay was still wet. Stamp seals remained in exclusive use during the Halaf period (in which the turn of the millennium may have taken place) and probably during the succeeding age, known as the Obeid. It was apparently in the next, or Uruk, period that cylindrical seals came into being. The new shape was favored by the added usefulness of having a seal that could be rolled without interruption for as great a distance as might be needed. This was not only desirable in the case of wide-mouthed storage jars but even more so in the case of storehouse doors that were to be sealed.

The Uruk age was culturally quite fruitful in producing still other innovations that were profoundly to affect all the subsequent Sumero-Accadian periods. The most spectacular innovation was the ziggurat or stage tower which gave rise to the Bible myth of the Tower of Babel and many examples of which have been excavated in Mesopotamia. But a still more significant contribution of the Uruk age was the invention of writing. This writing seems to have started out as a group of conventionalized pictures incised on seal cylinders. These pictographs were stylized into linear signs later on in the fourth millennium. During the first half of the third millennium they were further stylized into cuneiform. During the three millennia that preceded the Christian Era, contracting parties and their witnesses impressed their seals on millions of clay cuneiform tablets. The seal was tantamount to its owner's signature. It is interesting to note that the stamp seal is better suited for use on tablets than is the cylinder, because a little stamp takes less space, and on tablets space is usually at a premium. However, so great was the force of inertia that the cylinder continued to be the predominant type of seal, even for authenticating tablets, down to the Neo-Babylonian period, deep in the first millennium B.C., when the stamp eclipsed the cylinder, eventually expelling the usurper that had dominated the scene for three thousand years.

In its broad sense, "glyptic art" includes all sculpture.

Art historians, however, tend to restrict the term to the miniature sculpture of the seal cutter. Our discussion of glyptics will be limited to cylinders. The photographs tell most of the story. However, since the seals are not reproduced in color, I should perhaps note that they are usually made of stone. Certain stones tend to be used in certain periods. For example, lapis-lazuli is often the material of cylinders in the early tombs at Ur but not in Babylonia and Assyria of the first millennium B.C. The reverse is true of chalcedony. In addition to numerous kinds of stone; metal, shell, bone, frit, and other materials are sometimes used. I should also call the reader's attention to the piercing down the middle of the cylinder to serve primarily for inserting the roller and perhaps secondarily for suspension on the cord around the owner's neck. To appreciate the skill of the ancient gem cutters we should remember that they were able to depict a wealth of detail even though the height of the seals is normally only between one and two inches and though the stone is often quite hard. The minuteness of the workmanship is the more striking because the ancient gem cutters did not apparently know of the magnifying glass.

The Iraq Museum in Baghdad has one of the finest and largest collections of Mesopotamian glyptics in the world. This collection is growing more rapidly than its rivals and it will doubtless eclipse those in the Louvre and British Museum that may possibly be larger at present. In 1935, the Department of Antiquities of the Iraq Government invited me to undertake the publication of ancient seals. The few months I spent at the Museum in Baghdad in 1935, before I had to return to America, were of course not nearly enough for me personally to make impressions of the three thousand seals and to have them photographed. It is due to the enlightened interest of Saty Beg, the Director of Antiquities, and Abdu-r-Razzaq Lutfy Effendi, the Curator of the Museum, that preliminary impressions were made, photographed, and sent to me with the result that I at least could study the material without delay. After the present war I hope to return to Baghdad in order to make impressions and photographs that show a maximum of detail for every seal: such is the standard for scientific publications of art. Meanwhile, with the kind permission of Saty Beg, I have selected some of the clearer photographs now in my possession to illustrate glyptic art. Because all these seals come from Iraq, the peripheral glyptic types peculiar to the surrounding lands are not represented.

Obviously I cannot treat the subject of Western Asiatic glyptics (or even of the Iraq Museum seals alone) in detail here. My aim must be more modest. I propose to describe a selection of seals arranged in chronological order and show how cultural history may be extracted from them.

At the outset we ought to recognize the fact that while the seals were used for the practical purposes of indicating ownership and of authentication, the seal cutters regularly tried to make an artistic creation with aesthetic appeal. Functionally, the seal needed only the distinctiveness that a few aimlessly scratched lines would provide (and there are scattered examples of such). But, then again, the function of the seal would in no way be impaired by artistic merit. Actually, beauty would normally facilitate the sale of the seal cutter's products.

Some of the seals reproduced here (such as Nos. 18, 19, 31, 32) have a beauty that transcends the taste of those for whom they were made and appeal even to us, though we be far off in time and place. They are in my opinion as universal as art can be. We naturally prefer skill to ineptitude, composition to chaos, charm to drabness, vitality to deadness. But we must remember that an aesthetically inferior work of art may be of great value for the historian of culture (e.g., No. 16) while a handsome piece of an already known type may not even add anything to our knowledge of art.

The seals of the Uruk period are often characterized by a remarkable degree of movement. A lively specimen is No. 1 (the lower part of which is unfortunately broken away). A calf leaps in mid-air as if over the back of the humped bull in the foreground. The artists regularly take the necessary liberty with perspective so as to show both horns symmetrically. The calf's wavy, curved horns are gracefulness itself. A stylized tree provides the natural atmosphere. This seal dates from the second half of the fourth millennium B.C.

The Uruk period imperceptibly evolved into, and was not violently supplanted by, the Jemdet Nasr Age. No. 2 is a seal that may well mark the transition from Uruk to Jemdet Nasr. A nude hero grasps the tail of a lion to pull him off his prey, a bull. At the same time the hero shows

SEAL 1

SEAL 2

SEAL 3

SEAL 4

an apparently protective interest in a goat. Under the latter is a jar symbolizing fertility and plenty. A rather ineffectively conventionalized plant indicates the environment. This seal reflects an attitude of the early inhabitants of Babylonia, who were possibly the Sumerians: They had gotten beyond the hunting stage and had become herdsmen of large and small cattle. Thus the gem cutter often shows men rescuing cattle from beasts of prey, notably from the lion. The use of the drill is quite noticeable on this seal; note the circular drillings to indicate the hero's eye, the goat's hooves, and the jar. The drill is employed widely throughout the Jemdet Nasr age.

No. 3 is a Jemdet Nasr seal showing a bear attacking a bull. An eagle with spread wings soars overhead. A tree is in the background. In this period beasts tend to be sculptured as if their torsos consisted of three detachable parts. This seal is unusual in that the bear is rare in Mesopotamian art.

I consider No. 4 the handsomest example of fine art I know from the fourth millennium B.C. A tree growing on a conventionalized mountain provides the setting. While one deer reclines in the background, another in the foreground kneels to lap water from a stream. Inasmuch as deer are not otherwise shown lapping water, the artist may well have known from personal observation that the deer kneels on its forelegs to drink. Thus convention does not stifle the truly gifted artist.

The Jemdet Nasr seal cutters also fashioned cylinders with geometric and floral designs. On No. 5 are two different flowers; dotted circles are arranged symmetrically in the field. Above and below are borders with slant hatchings, between the end of the seal and a horizontal line.

No. 6 comes from the period of the early tombs at Ur; an age now called the Third Early Dynastic that fell sometime in the first half of the third millennium B.C. While to the inexpert eye this seal may at first appear enigmatic, the subject is quite clear. Two people seated on chairs are enjoying a drink together. They draw the beverage from the jar through copper tubes: the Sumerian equivalent of "straws." The social inferiority of the two attendants is mirrored in their small size. The crude representation of the face is a natural outgrowth of the technique in No. 2. Sumerian men are regularly shown clean-shaven of head as well as face, clad in a skirt, and nude from the waist up. The crescent moon in the upper center is so frequent a device that we need not point it out every time it will occur on the other seals. The jar incidentally is set on a stand.

Nos. 7-19 from the dynasty of Sargon of Accad, the first Semite to conquer the ancient world, date from the twenty-fifth and twenty-fourth centuries. No. 7 depicts the same subject as No. 6 but the style is quite different. The Accadian artist is far closer to reality than his Early Dynastic forerunner. Real men, rather than fantastic outlines, drink from the common jar. In accordance with Semitic notions of personal decorum, the drinkers and their attendant are clad in long robes that cover almost the whole body. The right shoulder is left

SEAL 5

SEAL 6

SEAL 7

SEAL 8

uncovered and free. The men have hair on their heads and generous beards in good Semitic fashion. The chairs are of the camp-stool variety. Incidentally, since chairs and other pieces of furniture were usually made of wood, and clothes of wool, the objects themselves have been long disintegrated by time and moisture. What we know of artifacts made of organic matter comes from artistic representations of, and literary references to them.

While No. 8 is not a great piece of art, it is nevertheless of interest as a clear representation of a typical theme. Antithetic, rampant lions attack a pair of crossed bulls. On each side, a hero wearing a flat cap plunges a dagger into the lion's neck with one hand and grasps the lion's tail with the other. The symmetrical composition is roughly in the shape of "I IXI I." The bulls' heads are shown in profile except for the horns that are in front view. The lions' heads are seen as if from above. A divine symbol terminates the scene.

No. 9 shows two similar heroes, one straddling a bull, the other a lion. The beasts seem to groan with open mouths, so painful are the tail-and-leg holds. As usual the Accadian artist produces a symmetrical scene. Note the crouching deer at the lower center. To the side is the panel with the owner's name. Our hero is often taken to be Gilgamesh, whose exploits are recounted in the greatest epic of pre-Homeric antiquity: The Gilgamesh Epic, about which we shall presently have more to say. But whether or not the hero is Gilgamesh, he is a well-defined personality in the artistic monuments. He is regularly shown face-front, but body in profile. He is nude except for a wrestling belt, on which holds were to be attached in conformity with the rules of an ancient school of wrestling. He is well bearded and his hair comes down in curls on either side. Jemdet Nasr (and perhaps Uruk) age artists depicted him at first with one curl on each side. Toward the close of the fourth millennium we find our hero with two curls on either side. By the Accadian period, however, and for all future times, he is regularly represented with three on a side. Usually a character antithetically duplicated does not imply the existence of twin heroes; the device is purely for symmetry. However, here the artist has differentiated the heroes; the one on the right has the normal three curls, and the one on the left, the atypical two. I do not know whether the differentiation is accidental or whether it will prove of significance mythologically.

No. 10 shows an antithetic repetition of the same hero vanquishing a bull that he has turned upside down and into whose neck he sinks a heel. Note the dagger fixed in the hero's belt. The miniature scene in the center delineates a minor deity (perhaps the apotheosized king) hailing the seated major god who welcomes him. The respective gestures these gods make with their hands are presumably those of the ancient Mesopotamians under similar circumstances. The horned crown indicates divinity; the numerous horns of the seated god show his exalted rank among the gods. His flounced robe is more splendid than the simpler dress of the lesser god. The seated god holds a flowing vase which may mean that he is Ea; see Nos. 13, 15. A horned quadruped

SEAL 9

SEAL 10

SEAL 11

SEAL 12

looking behind him stands under the inscribed panel. The bifurcation of his tail may be a device to give the illusion of motion; see the better example in No. 18.

Nos. 11 and 12 show the same hero vanquishing a bull and another hero, Enkidu by name, conquering a lion. There is no doubt about the identification of Enkidu, for he is described in the Gilgamesh Epic as he is represented on the seals. He is tauromorphous (i. e., like a bull) from the waist down and human from the waist up (except for bull's horns and ears). According to the Epic, Gilgamesh was the tyrant of the city of Uruk (Biblical Erech). His oppression caused his subjects to cry to the gods for help. In response the gods fashioned Enkidu out of clay. After a period of "training" in the wilds, where Enkidu protected weak animals from hunters and beasts of prey, he engaged in mighty combat with Gilgamesh. The battle ended in a tie, with both giants greatly impressed with each other's strength. They formed a bond of friendship and began a joint career of beneficent valor, in which they slew many wicked beasts and monsters the world over. Note the Accadian artists' device of showing the far elbow bent upwards so that both arms may be seen. In No. 11, the faintly visible panel is so placed as to add to the symmetry, whereas in No. 12 its poor location detracts from the symmetry. The metal ends of No. 12 are still preserved.

Accadian seals are rich in mythological scenes. No. 13 shows the "Zu-bird" brought for judgment before Ea, god of justice. Ea holds the vase from which flow the two sources of water. Possibly the duality of the streams was suggested by the two rivers of Mesopotamia: the Tigris and Euphrates. In any case even the far-off Canaanites later conceived of the underground water as "The Two Deeps." The deity in front of Ea is possibly a sort of divine prosecuting attorney (compare the role of Satan, as in the Book of Job). The defendant—bird below the waist, man above it—is brought in by a "divine policeman." The latter carries a club (of the mace type) and leads in the defendant by the scruff of his neck. The defendant is the Zu-bird about whom a myth has come down to us. He had stolen the "Tablets of Destiny" from heaven. The tablets, somewhat like the fruit of the Tree of Knowledge, could impart divine knowledge and power. The Zu-bird, who fled to the mountains, was so formidable a creature that most of the gods were afraid to go after him. He was apparently captured by a ruse. His wife was invited to a "heavenly" party with the result that jealousy brought the Zu-bird within reach of the divine police. The text is fragmentary and so the actual capture has not been preserved in writing. However, the art vividly shows the Zu-bird brought to justice. Thus do art and literature fill each other's gaps.

No. 14 is one of the most surprising revelations of modern archaeology. Two horned deities destroy a seven-headed monster, while a couple of men look on. The god in front of the monster has killed four of the heads but three heads are still alive and fighting. The body of the monster has gone up in flames and so his doom is sealed. There can be no doubt that this is a fore-

SEAL 13

SEAL 14

SEAL 15

SEAL 16

runner of the Grecian myth of Heracles and the seven-headed Hydra. Even in the Grecian version Heracles is assisted and the monster is destroyed by fire. This seal dates from about the twenty-fifth century B.C. long before the ancestors of the Greeks had reached Greece or emerged from barbarism. Nothing could be more striking than this illustration of the oriental origins of Greek culture. Recent discovery has shed more light on this myth. From the Ugarit myths we know that Leviathan was a seven-headed monster. (See p. 139.) The early Canaanites attributed his conquest to Baal; the Hebrews ascribed it to Yahweh.

No. 15 is a masterpiece of exquisite detail. Ea is seated in his ocean shrine. Fish may be seen above the streams issuing from his vase. Water completely surrounds his abode. He exchanges greetings with an astral deity who ascends the lofty mountain heights that are conventionalized as triangles. He also holds a mace (?). His celestial nature is implied by the rays that issue from one of his shoulders. Behind him rises the Sun god with sunshine streaming from both shoulders, and holding his symbol, the saw-toothed dagger. Behind the Sun god is the wing of eventide; before him, the wing of dawn over which he is about to rise. The wings are personified: the one as a lion whose head may be seen on careful observation, the other as a typical god with a crown of many horns. Behind the shrine kneels "Gilgamesh" holding a divine emblem. Here, as now and then in the seals, his face is atypically in profile with the side curls shown as if they were in back.

No. 16 speaks as eloquently as any text could on the religious concepts and usages of the times. A personage who may possibly be a priest hails the seated god as he introduces the devotee, whose hands are clasped in reverence. The god, whose divinity is as usual indicated by horns, is not purely anthropomorphic, for his nether parts are in the form of a snake. Snake worship is quite prominent throughout ancient Western Asia. The flames on the altar show that a sacrifice is being offered. The ear of grain tells us that the goal of the sacrifice is fertility.

No. 17 is another presentation and offering scene. The bareheaded, bearded worshiper brings a kid to his god. One minor deity leads the worshiper in by the hand, while another deity greets the seated god who holds a mace, and bespeaks good offices. The doctrine of intercession is common all through the ancient Near East and we shall hear more of it in the next chapter. The divine symbol known from No. 8 divides the scene. Overhead are the familiar heavenly devices of star and crescent moon. Before the god is what may be a many-legged altar.

Nos. 18 and 19 are models of charm. Beautiful friezes are made by continuous rollings of these seals. They are conventional but yet fresh. No. 18 shows crossed lions attacking rampant deer that look away behind them. The bifurcation of their tails gives an effective illusion of motion here. A date palm borders the scene. No. 19 depicts an eagle, with spread wings and great stylized tail, digging talons into antithetic deer that have risen to their

SEAL 17

SEAL 18

SEAL 19

SEAL 20

SEAL 21

hind legs but have not yet succeeded in getting up on their front legs. A tree terminates the scene.

With No. 20 we enter the age of the Third Dynasty of Ur, the last great period of Sumerian domination, in the twenty-second and twenty-first centuries B.C. The presentation scene is the favorite one of the times: a minor deity introduces the devotee to a seated god. The throne is set on a platform. The devotee is again clean-shaven in conservative Sumerian style. An eagle flies overhead. The inscription gives the name and title of the cupbearer who owned it.

No. 21 is in two registers. The upper scene is a sim-plified stylization of that in No. 20 while the lower is a freize of swans swimming on billowy water. The com-bination of scenes on a single seal by the same artist establishes their contemporaneousness; a fact that may be of importance to the art historian when the scenes are found individually on other seals.

No. 22 also depicts a minor deity introducing a wor-shiper to a god. The god is perched on his symbolic beast, the bull. He is perhaps to be identified as Adad, the storm god. His smallness is due to a trend against the portrayal of divinity. Indeed on some seals the god him-self is not depicted but is represented by his symbolic animal, supplemented by this god's emblem of forked lightning. The tendency to eliminate representations of the god is well known to the adherents of the great monotheistic religions. But even among ancient poly-theists the tendency is quite noticeable in different epochs. Thus the gods are frequently represented by

their symbols alone on Neo-Babylonian seals. It is therefore possible that the golden calves of the Northern
Kingdom of Israel, far from being worshiped for themselves, were conceived of simply as pedestals for the
unseen Yahweh. However, the Judean authors of the
Bible did not choose to see the religion of their Israelite
rivals in so harmless a light. The ostrich that stands before the bull is not uncommon on the seals of many
periods. The ostrich is still to be found in Western Asia
and I have seen one in the Syrian Desert.

No. 23 shows the devotee before the god, who sits on
a covered throne. The goddess frequently appears on
these seals with hands raised to bespeak a kindly recep-
tion. She is known from the mural paintings recently
discovered at Mari and dating from the days of the great
Hammurabi of the nineteenth century B.C. The murals
show that her flounced dress is covered with scallops of
many colors. This may be the type of formal robe that
Jacob gave his son Joseph: the "coat of many colors."
Behind the god, stands an attendant, before whom is a
squat monkey. Before the god is a mannikin (whose size
indicates small importance rather than small physical
stature). Back of the devotee is his name in cuneiform:
IGI-TA-NI. A "dragon-headed" symbol borders the
scene.

The Old Assyrian period falls mostly after the close of
the Third Dynasty of Ur, and is mainly contemporary
with the early part of the First Dynasty of Babylon (in
the first third of the second millennium B.C.). No. 24
is a characteristic Old Assyrian seal. While the treatment

SEAL 22

SEAL 23

SEAL 24

SEAL 25

SEAL 26

is quite different, the theme is a presentation scene of Third Dynasty type. A minor deity introduces the worshiper to the seated god. The gods have flounced robes; the worshiper wears a simple one. Both the worshiper and the god, who sits on a covered throne, have caps indicated by slant hatching. The subsidiary scene in two registers shows a bull above with a symbol over its back, and two marching mannikins below. There is a sun disc over a crescent moon between the gods. Old Assyrian seals and texts are generally called "Cappadocian" because most of them happen to have been found in the excavations in Asia Minor, where there were extensive colonies of Assyrian merchants. However, the Old Assyrian seals in the Iraq Museum come from Iraq itself and so are added proof that "Old Assyrian" is more accurate a description than "Cappadocian" for certain groups of these seals. Old Assyrian texts have also turned up in Assyria; e. g., in an early level under the Hurrian town of Nuzu.

No. 25 is a classical presentation scene of the First Dynasty of Babylon, of which Hammurabi is the outstanding king. All of the characters stand; even the major god. As often in this age, the worshiper offers a kid. The god is probably the Sun god, as the saw-toothed dagger suggests. He extends one foot through the slit of his long skirt and rests it on a pedestal. The goddess with raised hands blesses the occasion.

No. 26 shows a worshiper, in a short Amorite dress, in the presence of the same Sun god. The ancillary scene in two registers has three smaller figures standing below and three upside-down above. Below on the left is the nude woman (who represents fecundity), facing front and holding her breasts. To her right are a couple of dancing men. In the upper register to the left (i. e., when the seal has been inverted) is the "bandy-legged" man. Though his head is in profile, the rest of his body faces front. His view and posture are dictated by his nature: since he symbolizes the male part of fecundity, it is appropriate that his genitalia be visible. He raises a hand welcoming a nude man and a clad man who hail him.

No. 27 is another First Dynasty presentation scene. A lesser deity in a long robe introduces the devotee who wears a hunting skirt. The main god carries a hunter's throw-stick. The god's symbol, the crook of Amurru (the national god of the Amorites whose dynasty was ruling the land), is set on the ground before him, while the same symbol is placed on the face of the dog behind him. The additional symbols of a fish and a star are in the field.

After the fall of the First Dynasty, in the first half of the seventeenth century B.C., the land was ruled by the Cassites for about half a millennium. In spite of their general decadence, the Cassites ruled longer than any of the vigorous dynasties before or since. No. 28 is a Cassite seal in two registers and may date from around the middle of the second millennium B.C. In the upper scene the bird—apparently eating a plant held by the seated personage—placed above a rising bull may recall the winged shrine of some far earlier seals. The panel encloses the

SEAL 27

SEAL 28

SEAL 29

SEAL 30

name and title of the scribe who owned the seal. It is the lower register that is of primary interest. Three men are using an agricultural machine that plows and sows simultaneously. One man goads the yoke of oxen while another (with a conical hat) holds the plowshares down in the ground; the man in the middle is pouring seed into the funnel of the seeder. To the best of my knowledge this is the most sophisticated agricultural machine ever invented before the nineteenth century A.D. The Arab peasants today have nothing that compares with this machine of Cassite Babylonia.

The Middle Assyrian period covers the last four centuries of the second millennium B.C. No. 29 is an unusual example of Middle Assyrian glyptics and may be dated roughly to the thirteenth century B.C. Two graceful, rampant deer are held by a personified feature of landscape (perhaps a mountain). Out of the latter grow a couple of stylized trees. The scene is flanked by a palm tree on which are perched a pair of birds and on either side of which is a rosette. While the top part of the seal is unfortunately broken off, the bottom is bordered by a line of drilled dots that are interrupted only by the mountain (?) and the palm.

The remaining three seals are Late Assyrian, and date from about the eighth century B.C. No. 30 depicts a pair of winged sphinxes sitting antithetically about a conventionalized tree. The sphinx to the right is a bearded male; the one to the left is unbearded and probably female. Each raises a paw toward the tree. Overhead is the winged tailed sun disc of Assur, the national god. A rosette bounds the scene. The sphinxes reflect the Egyptian influence that was so strong in Late Assyrian times. It will be recalled that contacts with Egypt were strong throughout this period and that Egypt was even included in the Assyrian Empire during part of the seventh century B.C. This seal frankly lacks life. The next two seals, on the other hand, are full of motion.

No. 31 shows a winged, bird-headed griffon menacing a deer that looks behind in its flight. The theme is not original with the artist but he handles it with consummate skill. The high degree of stylization does not interfere with the illusion of speed. The sloping axis is an integral factor in attaining this effect.

No. 32 shows an Assyrian hunter pursuing a deer and discharging his arrows at it. The deer, already transfixed by a couple of shafts, looks back in its rapid flight. The fish in the field symbolize the concept of plenty. The artist does not mean to convey the impression that the hunter is directly behind the deer. There is not enough room on these cylinders to show the space between the hunter and the deer. The ancient artists counted on the imagination of the spectator to supply so simple a detail.

Perhaps the best way for me to convey an idea of the vastness and importance of the ancient art of Western Asia is to remind you that the foregoing cylinders are but a shade over 1 per cent of the seals in a single museum; that glyptics is only one of many branches of the art; that most of the unearthed material is still unpublished; and that all of the unearthed material is probably less than 1 per cent of what is still under ground.

SEAL 31

SEAL 32

CHAPTER VII

THE GODS AND HEROES
OF UGARIT

ONE OF the most fascinating periods in history is the Amarna Age, which flourished in the fifteenth and fourteenth centuries B.C. It was an age of great internationalism, when the Pharaohs of Egypt were in active correspondence with the kings of Western Asia and of the islands of the East Mediterranean. The period is attested by the most important and interesting group of inscriptions that has come down to us from antiquity: the Tell el Amarna letters, containing the personal correspondence of those kings. It is interesting that as recently as the winter of 1933-34 the Egypt Exploration Society discovered eight new cuneiform documents at Tell el Amarna. I had the good fortune to be called to Cairo to interpret and prepare for publication these new tablets. My manuscript is at present in London, and I do not know what has happened to it; but in any case it will probably not appear before the end of the war. Six of the eight new tablets are school texts and exercises from the local academy where Egyptians were taught to read and write the international language, Babylonian. However, the two most interesting texts are letters. One is the record-office copy of the Pharaoh's letter introducing his new royal commissioner of Ascalon, Palestine, to the governor of that city. The other letter was sent to the Pharaoh by a Syrian chieftain, who writes of invasions, burnings and slaughter in his district. He claims, with more apparent than real sincerity, to be loyal to the Pharaoh; but he was probably looking out for his own interests and may even have been using the same tactics to ingratiate himself with the Hittite king, Pharaoh's rival. Egypt was in the course of losing its Asiatic empire in the Amarna Age.

The Amarna Age is known to us not only from the Tell el Amarna letters but also by several interesting groups of documents found in Mesopotamia, in Asia Minor, and lately in North Syria. A remarkable group was unearthed within the last twelve years at the ruins of Ugarit on the North Syrian coast. Ugarit has long been known to us by name from other records. But it came to light as an actual city through one of the merest coincidences. Toward the end of 1928 an Arab peasant discovered a tomb there, quite by accident. The discovery soon reached the ears of archaeologists, and within a few months a French expedition was organized to excavate Ugarit. In 1929, after a few weeks of digging, the expedition came across a temple, with archives; and lo and behold, they were written in a hitherto unknown script: cuneiform, but apparently alphabetic and unlike Mesopotamian cuneiform. This writing proved to be a completely new type of script and to embody a new category of literature. The tablets were turned over to a distinguished French cuneiformist, Charles Virolleaud, who in 1929 published 48 of the texts and later identified some of the letters. The fewness of the signs showed that the script was alphabetic, for no other system of writing, such as the syllabic or the logographic systems, would have so few characters: only about 30 altogether.

This new writing might conceivably have been used to record an entirely new language; but the original investigators worked on the assumption that the language would be Canaanite; that is to say, akin to Phoenician and Hebrew. This assumption turned out to be correct. Hans Bauer, a German scholar, brilliantly identified many of the letters. His work was checked and added to by a Frenchman, Edouard Dhorme, who had a long record of splendid decipherment work behind him. Virolleaud practically completed the alphabet. During the first World War Père Dhorme was engaged in decoding messages intercepted from the Central Powers, which shows that even a specialist in ancient oriental languages can as such be of use to his country in war time.

The Ugaritic documents were studied also by many other scholars in many different lands, and now we can interpret not less than 50 per cent of the unbroken passages: a remarkable achievement particularly because the available texts were only published from 1929 to as recently as 1938.

The texts themselves are of varied content. Some are letters, others are business documents, others are rituals, others are temple records of various kinds. But the great bulk of them are poetic texts recording, so to speak, the lives of the North Canaanite gods, known to us from the Old Testament as the pagan gods that Yahweh's people were not to worship. We have, then, the reverse side of the Hebrew religion: the biography of the gods of the forbidden religion that preceded, and also existed side by side with, the religion of the Israelites.

The texts deal mostly with the gods, and to some extent with human heroes. The gods of Ugarit are anthropopathic; that is, they are subject to human emotions and if you have a lofty concept of divinity, you will not find these gods behaving as gods should. They eat, they drink, they love, and they fight like human beings; and often like human beings at their worst. In form, the gods are usually anthropomorphic, having the shape of men. Sometimes they are even theriomorphic, having the shape of animals. But in spite of their crudeness, we can detect in them rudiments of virtues, human and divine, which form the background—the prehistory as it were—of the human and divine virtues that we now respect. For instance, of the hero Daniel, the favorite of Baal, it is written that he spends his time judging the cause of the widow and orphan—in perfect Old Testament wording. Again, it is said that Baal (in one of his more moral moments) abhors the sacrifices of wickedness. Here too the thought and form are duplicated in the Old Testament and we are reminded especially of some of the prophecies of Amos.

As for the gods themselves: The father of men and gods is El, who is G/god with either small or capital "g." The Hebrew word *el* similarly denotes either "God" or "god." El dwells in a land whence the two "deeps" surge. These two deeps break through the crust of the earth, giving us springs and fountains. One of El's epithets is "creator of creatures." His character is mild. He is always pleasant; never in a rage. He never interferes with the normal activities of nature; but the other gods always come to him when decisions must be made, for he is the supreme authority.

His wife is Asherah, one of the goddesses whom we find abused in the Old Testament. Her epithet is "creatress of the gods." She bore to El a brood of seventy gods and goddesses, among whom are numbered the most active personalities of this pantheon. The most colorful of her sons is Baal, who dwells in the mountain of the north, in Sapan. He is the nature god, who dies with the passing of the rains every spring and comes to life with their renewal in the autumn. His epithet is "the rider of clouds"—an epithet which is actually applied to Yahweh in one of the Psalms.

The most colorful goddess is Anat, goddess of love and war. She is the most bloody of all the warriors in the pantheon. Her devotion to her lover Baal transcends even death, as we shall see.

There are many others: Kathar-wa-Hasis is the Vulcan of the Ugaritic gods, the craftsman and artificer who fashions everything from beautiful jewelry to palaces fit for the gods.

There is a whole brood of lesser gods, among them some who are mere lackeys of the great gods, and are fit for nothing but to do menial services, such as to prepare donkeys for the gods to ride upon or to bear messages from deity to deity.

Many of the doings of the gods are on the shocking side. One may also find the hyperbole and the strangeness of the poetic idiom a little jarring to our sense of the aesthetic and literary. Furthermore, one must not expect to find the rules of this world at work: The gods of Ugarit live in an entirely different world and are subject to different rules of nature. But if you are willing to forget this mad world of the twentieth century A.D. and let me lead you back to the reign of the good King Niqmed of Ugarit, we shall peep into the lives of the Ugaritic gods and heroes.

The first glimpse that we have of the theogony is in a tablet that tells of the creation of the "beautiful and gracious gods." We do not know how El created his two wives, but we see him with them, kissing their lips sweet as grapes. They conceived and produced Shahar, the morning star; and his brother, Shalem. They are only babies to the gods of Ugarit, but compared with us mortals they are giants indeed; for no sooner are they weaned than they stretch one lip to the heaven and the other to the earth, so that they devour both the fowl of the air and the fish of the sea; and on this nourishment they attain mature godhood. Of the birth of the seventy sons of Asherah we do not yet know. Perhaps further excavations will reveal more tablets to fill this gap. From the creation of the second generation of the gods, we turn to one of the main cycles of the Ugaritic pantheon:

the Baal cycle, the epic of the great dying god of fertility. If my presentation of this material seems a little choppy, the chief reason is that the tablets are not consecutive. Some tablets are still missing while many of those we have are broken. Furthermore, we are able to translate only half of the legible material. But the remarkable thing is not that half cannot yet be read, but that half *can* be read; and with certainty after so short a time.

The god of death, or infertility, is Mot. We find him instructing Baal how to vanquish Leviathan, the seven-headed monster of the sea. The epithets which describe Leviathan (as well as his name itself) are those of the Old Testament, word for word. That is to say, they are not merely the same in translation; they are exactly the same words, just as English "man" and German "Mann" not only mean the same thing but are the same word. And as Baal slays Leviathan in the Ugaritic mythology, so too Yahweh slays the seven-headed monster in the Hebrew mythology.

After the vanquishing of Leviathan, we come across another episode in Baal's career. He is mated with a heifer, who bears him a bull calf and Baal rejoices greatly on being blessed with this son.

We don't know how Baal met his death, but we read of him lying prostrate in a field, dead. When El hears this, he steps first from his throne to his footstool, then from his footstool to the ground, and there he sits and covers his head with the "dust of mourning" and girds himself with sackcloth. Anat hears of it also, and rushes to the scene of her dead lover Baal. She asks the sun goddess to place him on her (Anat's) shoulders so that she may fly with him to Sapan, the mountain home of Baal. There she buries him and mourns for him and, with all the generosity of a goddess, offers sacrifices: beasts, not by ones and twos but by seventies, as a memorial for Baal.

Then the gods are confronted with the problem of who is to rule the earth in Baal's stead. Anat comes to El and his wife Asherah, and says that they may rejoice, for another child of theirs is to be selected to rule the world. They consider several sons of Asherah, but all are ruled out for one reason or another. Finally their son Athtar the Terrible becomes Lord of the Earth and exercises sovereignty over the world.

We next find Mot, the god of death, speaking to Anat. He tells her that it was he who killed her lover Baal. She has been looking for revenge and she takes it. The text reads:

> *With a sword she cleaves him*
> *With a pitchfork she winnows him*
> *With fire she burns him*
> *In the millstones she grinds him*
> *In the field she plants him.*

And thus she avenges the death of her lover Baal.

But do not be surprised to find that not only Baal will reappear on the scene again, but Mot also. Because among the gods of old Ugarit, death is not irrevocable, and the dead can be brought back to life.

People as well as gods are informed or warned of things through dreams that El sends them. But now El himself has a dream, and it gives him an insight into an event that he had not known of. El dreams that:

> *The heavens rain oil*
> *The wadies run with honey.*

In other words, nature is plentiful again, and this means that somehow Baal, god of fertility, has been brought back to life. Anat is overjoyed at the news, and goes out to search for her beloved Baal. The theme of searching for one's beloved is familiar to us from the Song of Songs, and still characterizes the love stories and love songs of the Arabs to this day.

En route Anat meets the sun goddess and asks her if she has seen Baal. She says she has not, but she is willing to help and so joins in the search. When the sun goddess finds Baal, he is back fighting with Mot. Both of them have come back to life and are again engaged in ferocious combat, biting like serpents and kicking like steeds. The sun goddess warns Mot that he had better be careful, for if El finds out what he is doing to Baal he will take away Mot's sovereignty and deprive Mot of his throne. This part of the story ends here with a break in the tablet.

The next incident is of added interest because we have a direct analogy in the Old Testament. Baal has no house but wants one so as to be like the other gods who have homes and palaces. (This recalls the arguments for the building of Yahweh's temple, and we find remarkable similarities in detail. The king of Israel, David, has his palace, and is it right that God should live in a tent? No, God also must have a house.) Anat finds out about this desire of Baal for a house, and wants to get El's permission to have one constructed. But they never do anything directly. They go first to one or more lesser lights, and so finally get to the important personage who has the ultimate word. Anat therefore goes to Asherah, who promises her that she will intercede and ask El's permission to build Baal's palace. Asherah tells her lackey Qadesh-Amrar to get ready her donkey and to put on the saddle and harness. He obeys, and he lifts his mistress, the Queen Asherah, onto the donkey, whereupon she rides off to the domain of El, at the source of the two deeps. El is quite agreeable. In fact, El never refuses a request; but yet his permission must always be asked. He says, yes indeed, Baal will have a palace; and not just a plain palace, but one of gold and silver. Anat is overjoyed, and goes to Baal to tell him the good news. The mountains co-operate, and supply great quantities of silver and gold. Then Baal and Anat go to consult the "Vulcan" of the gods, Kathar-wa-Hasis, and decide on the specifications for the palace. Kathar-wa-Hasis suggests to Baal the desirability of having windows in his palace. Baal at first withholds permission but is eventually won over. It is built, as Yahweh's temple was, of the cedars of Lebanon.

The next episode is one that I do not understand, although I can translate it literally. A fire burns the palace for six days and nights, and only on the seventh day does

The farming implements of the Arab peasant today are far less developed than the plowing-and-sowing machine of Cassite Babylonia (see seal 28 in Chapter VI). Here is a Syrian farmer tilling the soil with a primitive plow drawn by a humped ox. In the distance are the snowy Lebanons.

Syrian boys on their donkeys. Little donkeys such as those on which the goddess Asherah and the hero Daniel rode are still quite common in the Near East.

it depart, whereupon the palace is of gold and silver. Precisely what this means I do not know. Perhaps the precious metal was first overlaid on wood and when the wood was then burned away the silver and gold would be left in place. Perhaps magic was at work to adorn Baal's house by some supernatural effect of fire. In any case, the house is completed, and Baal gives a big feast for his brothers and sisters, the seventy offspring of Asherah. At this feast, as at all such feasts, a great many fatlings are slain, and there are generous servings of wine, amidst rejoicing.

Sometime thereafter Baal goes on a rampage and conquers not less than ninety cities. The last we hear of Baal, he is back fighting with Mot and goodness knows what is to happen to him. Perhaps he is to meet his death.

According to still another tablet, Baal had to kill the great sea god, the dragon Yamm. Kathar-wa-Hasis fashions two clubs for Baal, one called "Driver" and the other "Expeller," that are to swoop like eagles in the hands of Baal. With "Driver" he strikes Yamm on the back and drives him from his throne; with the other, "Expeller," he strikes Yamm on the head and expels him from the seat of his authority. (Yamm's throne and seat are one; the duality is required by the characteristic poetic parallelism.) So Baal uses the creations of Kathar-wa-Hasis with good effect, and Yamm collapses and falls to the earth.

Parallel to the Baal cycle is another series of tablets which the scribe himself calls the Anat tablets. These describe the doings of Anat and Baal, and there is some overlapping and even some contradiction between the two cycles; but in the world that we are discussing, there is no rule against paradoxes.

In the first column of the first tablet we see Baal served a fatling and much wine. He eats his fill and drinks pitchers of wine not only by the thousand but even by the myriad. Thereupon he breaks into pleasant song. What we call thunder was "the goodness of Baal's voice" to Ugarit's bards. And after Baal has sung his song, he decides to go to Sapan, his mountain dwelling. Here his heart is gladdened by the sight of his three beautiful daughters. There the tablet is broken off.

The next column tells of Anat, Anat exulting in battle, slaying the human beings who dwell on the shores of the Mediterranean, wading through blood to her knees and striding in gore to her hips, exulting in her heart and rejoicing in her liver. After exulting in battle and satisfying herself with slaughter, she washes up; and whenever she does this she washes with "the dew of heaven, the fat of earth, and the rain of the rider of clouds."

Then we find Baal sending an invitation to Anat, through a messenger who also bears a gift of precious gems for her bosom. These are the words of the messenger inviting her to come and find out Baal's great secret:

> *I have a word and I shall tell it to thee*
> > *An utterance and I shall declare it to thee:*
> *The word of the tree*
> > *The whisper of the stone*

The murmuring of the heavens to the earth
  The humming of the stars;
I have created lightning that the heavens may know,
  The word, that men may know
And that the multitudes of the earth may under-
  stand....
  Come and I shall show it to thee in my mountain.

Thus Anat receives the invitation to visit Baal in Sapan. When Anat reaches the mountain, he sets before her an ox, apparently prepared to be eaten. And again she washes in "the dew of heaven, the fat of earth, and the rain of the rider of clouds." After this peaceful feast at Baal's abode on the top of Sapan, another tablet goes on to tell of the house which Anat desires to give to Baal. Again Anat goes to El to get his permission, which El grants the more easily after she praises his wisdom, telling him that his words are wisdom itself. He grants her request. Whereupon Asherah sends her lackey Qadesh-Amrar to Egypt, where Kathar-wa-Hasis has his workshop. There at his bellows he stands fashioning his cunning metal work. And it is not surprising that he located in Egypt, where the finest crafts of that day were fostered.

So much for the main episodes of the main gods. There are minor episodes of lesser personages. For example, Yarih the moon god is in love with the goddess Nikkal. They are destined to be wed because El has predicted that they are to produce a wonderful son. Like the beginning of the Iliad or Aeneid, the poet begins with "I sing of Nikkal." We then learn that the Moon sends Hirihbi, the king of summer, to ask Baal for the hand of Nikkal in marriage. He offers a generous bride price of one thousand shekels of silver, even ten thousand shekels of gold. And he adds these words to the intermediary—for there must always be an intermediary in such delicate matters:

> *I shall send gems of lapis-lazuli*
> *I shall make her fields into vineyards*
> *The field of her love into orchards.*

This is the way he promises to be a good husband. Then comes the wedding ceremony, with everything arranged in order. The family stands around the scales. The father sets the beam, while the mother tends the trays of the balances; the sisters take care of the weights, while the brothers count the lumps of precious metal. The bride price is weighed carefully, down to the last shekel. After these formalities are over, the couple is wedded with a song to the divine songstresses, the Kathirat, and with this song the tablet ends.

This marriage of the gods is interesting to students of human institutions, because the terminology and the procedure are those of earthly weddings in Canaan. Of course one must use judgment in handling material of this kind, and not assume, for instance, that the price of a mortal bride was a thousand shekels of silver, ten thousand shekels of gold! But there is no doubt that the marriages that took place in heaven were patterned after those on earth.

Another tablet actually deals with a marriage of human beings. There was a king named Keret, who had paid the marriage price for the beautiful princess Haraya, daughter of King Pebel. Pebel had apparently changed his mind about his future son-in-law, and withheld Haraya from him and refused to allow her to join her betrothed, King Keret. Just as in ancient Troy, this meant war. For in those days wars were fought for beautiful women as well as for land and for economic advantage. For a reason that escapes us, Keret is faced with the prospect of the extinction of his clan. Keret upon learning this retired to his chamber and wept on a heroic scale: his tears dropped earthward like shekels, and his bed was wet with his weeping. He finally sobbed himself to sleep. In a dream El descended to him and revealed to him the course of events and what he was to do to gain possession of Haraya who would bear him progeny. He told him Pebel was going to make him a peace offering if he would give up the girl and retire to his own territory; and he disclosed what the necessary ritual was to bring Baal down from heaven and get Baal's support in winning the fair Haraya. Then Keret awoke and did what the god had revealed. He washed and rouged himself, offered sacrifices and poured libations. He ascended to the top of a tower, raised his hands heavenward, sacrificed to El and brought down Baal from heaven. He provided food for an expedition of six months, and set out with three million men, marching not only by twos and threes but even by thousands and myriads. They started off on the week's march to Udm, the land of King Pebel. After three days of marching, our hero came to a shrine of Asherah, here called "Asherah of the Tyrians, even the goddess of the Sidonians"; and he made this vow:

> *If I may take Haraya to my house,*
> *Yea cause the lass to enter my court,*
> *I will give twice her (weight) in silver*
> *Even thrice her (weight) in gold.*

Then he marches on, and at the end of the week (i.e., after four more days of marching), they reach Udm.

Just as Jonah was asleep at the crucial moment, Pebel —who seems to be something of a comic character—slept while three million men tramped up to his gates. But he woke up at:

> *The sound of the neighing of his steed*
> *The braying of his donkey*
> *The lowing of his plowing ox*
> *And the barking of his dog.*

He sent out a messenger to induce Keret to accept terms, and this was the message conveyed:

> *So says King Pebel:*
> *Take silver and gold*
> *A share of her estate*
> *And permanent slaves, horsemen and*
> *chariots . . . !*
> *Take many peace offerings!*
> *But begone, O King, from my house;*
> *Be distant, O Keret, from my court!*

But Keret replies that he has all these things: he has plenty of gold and silver and slaves; he does not want what he has already got:

> *But what is not in my house shalt thou give!*
>   *Give me Lady Haraya*
> *The well-bred, thy first born,*
>   *Whose charm is the charm of Anat*
> *Whose loveliness is the loveliness of Astarte*
>   *Whose neck is like lapis-lazuli*
> *And whose eyes are like alabaster [?] bowls...*
>   *Let me find repose in the gaze of her eyes.*
> *For in a dream El has given,*
>   *In a vision, the Father of Man,*
> *An offspring unto Keret*
>   *Yea, a lad to the servant of El.*

The marriage is inevitable because El has foreseen that they will not only be married but will produce a distinguished son. So Keret follows El's instructions and refuses Pebel's peace offering. Apparently the will of the gods is fulfilled eventually though the end of the text has not yet come to light.

A second part of the Keret Epic, according to Virolleaud (his full publication has not reached us because of the war; it was ready for publication about the time of the fall of France), is a picture of Keret in his old age. He is lying sick on his bed, and is apparently desirous of immortality. One of his sons tells him that he is not to be immortal, but to die like other men.

Another human hero who figures in these tablets is

one who is mentioned in the book of Ezekiel and in the apocryphal History of Susanna, the hero Daniel. (See p. 17.) This is not the Daniel famous for his exploits in the lions' den. This Daniel is another virtuous man, who spends his time seeing that justice is given to the widow and the orphan. Daniel's wife is the lady Danataya, and their happiness would be complete except that they are childless. The poem relates how Daniel is giving the gods food and drink. In fact, he feeds them and gives them drink for a week, so that they will become his friends. At last Baal intercedes on Daniel's behalf with the superior god, El. El is as usual quite amenable, and blesses Daniel, instructing him as to the proper ritual. For if men know the proper ritual and are blessed by the gods, all things are possible. In fulfillment of El's prediction, Danataya bears Daniel a son, who is called Aqhat. Daniel is elated and laughs:

> *He sets his feet on the footstool*
> *He raises his voice and shouts:*
> *I shall sit and rest*
> *And my soul shall repose in my breast.*
> *For a son is born unto me as unto my brethren*
> *Yea a root as unto my kin.*

Then he goes on and says what his son is going to do, and what his son is going to mean to him. Aqhat is going to perform all the domestic, religious and personal services for which a man needs a son. One of the personal services is described in this way:

> *To hold my hand when I am drunk*
> *My arm when I am sated with wine.*

He is thus eventually to have a grown-up son to take him home at night when necessary.

After the birth of his boy, Daniel invites to his house the songstresses, the Kathirat, the daughters of the New Moon. They eat and drink and sing for an entire week and then depart. Meanwhile, Aqhat grows up to be a fine young man and a powerful hunter. And one day Daniel, while dispensing judgment in the gate and protecting the widow and the orphan, lifts up his eyes and sees Kathar-wa-Hasis coming bearing a bow in his hands. Daniel thereupon closes court and invites the god to his tents. When they get there he instructs his wife Danataya to prepare food and drink for the god. Kathar-wa-Hasis hands over the bow, which is ultimately to be given to Aqhat. Having partaken of Daniel's hospitality, the god departs from the tents of his host. A short time thereafter, while Aqhat is out hunting, the goddess Anat sees him and is envious of the bow which enables him to hunt so well. He tells her that if she wants a bow she should go to Kathar-wa-Hasis who will perhaps make her one also. But Aqhat will not part with his own bow. She tries to persuade him by promising him what men have always wanted, immortality:

> *I'll make thee immortal and give thee power*
> *I'll make thee count years with Baal*
> *Thou shalt count months with the son of El.*

But he is not impressed and replies that he knows he is mortal, and is going to die some day. He refuses to give her his bow. But it is always dangerous for mortals to disobey the gods. Anat laughs sarcastically and tells Aqhat his fate is sealed. These are her words:

> *I shall meet thee on the path of sin—*
> *I shall humble thee on the path of pride.*

For being so haughty with a goddess, his doom is nigh.

But Anat does not dare do anything unless she gets permission from the father of gods, El. She goes to him and makes her appeal, which apparently is granted, though the tablet breaks off here.

In the next scene we find Anat resorting to a sort of violence that we might associate with Chicago gangsters of several years ago. She goes to an assassin, Yatpan, and plots the murder of the hapless Aqhat, the son so dear to his father Daniel. She tells Yatpan that she will fly with him in the midst of a flock of eagles and poise him above Aqhat's head just as the latter is sitting down to lunch in the open. Yatpan is then to strike Aqhat twice on the head and thrice on the ear, so that he will be killed and her honor will be avenged.

The assassination took place at a city called Qart Abilim, where Aqhat was hunting. She gave the signal, and Yatpan assassinated him according to the plan:

> *His soul went out like wind;*
> *Like a puff, his spirit;*
> *Like smoke out of his body.*

Thus did Aqhat perish.

Aqhat had a sister named Paghat. Upon hearing the tragic news, she was distraught and went into mourning. Daniel too was heart-broken. But there is little avail in grief alone; there are always things to be done. So Paghat harnesses his donkey, fits it with saddle and bridle, places Daniel on the donkey and sends him off to retrieve the body of his son. Now Daniel had heard that the eagles had devoured the corpse of his child, and when he finally spied the flock of eagles he raised his voice and shouted:

> *May Baal break the wings of the eagles,*
>   *May Baal break their pinions!*
> *Let them fall at my feet!*
>   *I shall split them open and look.*
> *If there is fat*
>   *If there is bone*
> *I shall weep for him and bury him;*
>   *I shall put him in the niche of the ghosts of*
>   *the earth.*

This imprecation is enough to get Baal to smash the wings of the eagles. Daniel opens them, but behold there is no fat and no bone within. So he invokes Baal again —this time to heal the eagles, for he had made a mistake. Baal mends the eagles and when their wings are made whole, Daniel cries: "Eagles, flee and fly!" And the flock is off again. Then Daniel lifts his eyes and beholds Hargab, father of the eagles. By the same imprecation, he brings Hargab to earth and opens him and looks inside; but finds nothing, and so Hargab is healed and sent off. Finally (the Semitic storyteller well knew the technique of suspense) Daniel beholds Semel, mother of the eagles. He brings her down by the help of Baal. She too falls at his feet. He opens her and finds fat and bone. He removes them and buries the body of his son. He raises his hands heavenward and cries: "May Baal break the wings of the eagles if they fly over the grave of my son." Then he goes to Qart Abilim, the town where the murder was perpetrated, and curses it with years of drought and famine:

> *Seven years may Baal fail,*
> *   Even eight, the rider of clouds!*
> *(Let there be) no dew,*
> *   No rain*
> *No surging of the two deeps*
> *No goodness of Baal's voice!*

And he weeps for seven years, and only after seven years does he dismiss the weeping women from his house, whereupon he makes sacrifices.

Meanwhile, Paghat has not been inactive. She vows that she is going to kill the slayer of her brother. Armed with a sword, and possibly disguised, she goes to Yatpan, the assassin among the gods, who after his tongue has been loosened with wine, brags of his crime. We may infer that she wreaks dire vengeance on him, even as Anat had done on Mot. But our tablet is broken off, and that is all we know of the legend of Aqhat.

You may believe, if you like, that there is a happy ending, because the story is called not the epic of Daniel (as some scholars say) but the epic of Aqhat. And in one of the Ezekiel passages Daniel is mentioned with two other righteous men, Noah and Job. God is represented as saying that even if these three men were here today they would escape only with their own lives but they would not save their children. We know that Noah saved his children, and Job came through with children (though not the same children he had before his ordeal). It would seem to follow that Daniel saved his son too. So it is quite possible, if that makes you feel any better, that Aqhat is brought back to life in a part of the legend yet to be found.

While the Ugaritic tablets are of considerable importance for their connections with the poetry of the Bible, and to a lesser extent with the Homeric epics and the literature of other ancient peoples, their main interest rests on their own merit as literature. They constitute a new chapter in the history of literature and in my opinion are the most important addition to ancient literature since the decipherment of Egyptian hieroglyphic and Mesopotamian cuneiform in the last century.

CHAPTER VIII

PRIVATE AND PUBLIC LIFE
IN NUZU

IN 1925 the attention of the American Schools of Oriental Research was directed to the mound of Nuzu in northeastern Mesopotamia. Excavations there continued till 1931, and in the course of excavation, many thousands of tablets were uncovered, nearly all dating from the Amarna Age, the fifteenth and fourteenth centuries B.C. These tablets give us the most intimate picture that we have found to date, of any community in remote antiquity.

The tablets deal with four or five generations. To take a specific family, the earliest-mentioned generation is represented by Turshenni. Then, the first generation to be attested as active in the city of Nuzu is represented by his son, Puhishenni. During his day the local king of Arrap-ha (the ancient name of Kirkuk, which city is now famous for its oil fields) was Kipteshup; while the mayor of Nuzu was Ili-Erish. The second active generation is marked by the career of the greatest known "hero" of the town, a man with the exotic Hurrian name of Tehiptilla. During his time, the local king was It-hiya; while the mayor, a scandalous character of whom we shall

156

hear more later, was Kushiharbe. The third active Nuzu generation of that family is represented by Ennamati, and the fourth by Takku, who lived to see the final doom of Nuzu.

Nuzu was a small town, but the villas of several "millionaires" happened to be located in this town. The archives of these millionaires were uncovered in the course of excavation and constitute the Nuzu tablets.

The texts are on clay tablets, written in a provincial dialect of Babylonian. Babylonian was not in fact the native language of these people. They were Hurrians of whom we have already had something to say. The texts were written to a great extent by Hurrian scribes who had learned Babylonian. Things being what they were, it is not surprising that the tablets include from time to time loan words in the native language, which furnish one of the keys to the Hurrian tongue. In a Babylonian text of fifty or sixty words, for example, there might be one or two Hurrian words and the context often provides the clue to the meaning of the loan words in the imperfectly known Hurrian language. All but two of the personal names mentioned above are not Semitic or Indo-European but native Hurrian names. (Only Ili-Erish is Semitic; while Kushiharbe is Cassite.)

In some ways, the Babylonian people, and the neighbors who came under their influence, were more tidy about their daily lives than we. All their transactions, no matter how trivial, had to be recorded and witnessed and sealed; as these imperishable clay tablets attest. The documents included in these private archives are of all sorts—accounts of transactions of sale, loan, exchange; marriage, adoption, and divorce; legal documents and court transactions of all kinds. Their lives are often far better documented than those of most of us.

The archives that are most numerous and particularly famous among scholars are the archives of the aggressive Tehiptilla; those of Shilwateshup, son of the king; and the archives of a grasping and successful business woman named Tulpunnaya, about whom we shall have more to say.

If morals are to be drawn from the study of life in Nuzu, they are that debt is dangerous, if not fatal, and that human frailty will find a way to thwart the wisdom of laws, no matter how wisely and carefully they are drawn up.

The documents are, as I said, of several types. I am going to sketch some of the main types, because they expose to us the social patterns to be traced in the town of Nuzu.

Many of the documents relate to exchange. Exchange, again, is of several types. There is, first, absolute exchange, by which A exchanges land for an equivalent parcel of land belonging to B. This is a permanent exchange, and the properties are not to revert back to the original owners. In addition the Nuzians resorted to temporary exchange. For instance, if A has a donkey and needs barley or metal, and B has barley or metal and needs the services of a donkey, they may effect an exchange either for a stipulated period, or with the pro-

viso that as soon as one man returns the barley or
metal, he may take back the donkey.

Coins, of course, were not in use, and whenever they
write of buying a thing with metal, the silver (or other
metal) is specified in terms of weight; and at that usually
an equivalent of value in nonmetal was intended: one-
half talent of silver was equal to an ox, an ass, and ten
sheep. There are also less standard equivalents in other
"denominations."

There are many documents relating to adoption.
Adoption played a very significant role in the society of
the ancient Near East. People for practical, social, and
religious reasons, had to have heirs. If a couple remained
childless for long, they would eventually adopt a free-
born child, or even a slave. For the continuity of the
estate was essential for the integrity of the social system;
an heir had to be secured in one way or another. Furthermore, the religion required that the members of a
family be on hand to take care of the burial and the
mourning rites of the dead. For many reasons, then,
adoption was indicated by the matrix of society. Those
adoptions also took the place of insurance and annuities
in our form of civilization. Thus, if a person was unmarried, or married but childless, with no son to look
after him in his old age, take care of the house and the
food supply, and manage the estate, he (she or they)
could adopt a son who would be bound legally to show
him filial respect, to take care of him in old age, to provide food, clothing, and shelter as long as he lived, to
bury and mourn for him when the time came, and to

keep the estate running. In exchange for this service, the adopted son becomes a member of an established household and thus his fortune is made. It really is a sort of social security or annuity provision. To take a specific example: A lady belonging to the class of palace maids (which means that she was in the service of the king) and apparently unmarried, made over her furniture and her slaves (including a marriageable woman) in return for the filial service of a young man who agreed not only to treat her with the respect due to a mother during all her life, but eventually to bury her and mourn properly for her. The adopted son in addition to getting the security and backing needed to be a "solid citizen" also gets a wife for himself in the person of the marriageable slave. There was thus mutual benefit, and no possible exception can be taken to such a social procedure.

Another lady, named Mattiya, owned seven "homers" of land, a tidy little stretch of property. But she had no son nor anyone else to look after her when she would become old. So she turned over her seven homers of land to Tehiptilla, who was perhaps the richest man of the community, and thereby adopted him. He was the richer for the land, and she had the security of being taken care of for life by the Henry Ford or the John D. Rockefeller of her community.

Of course there were slaves as well as free men, and there was an almost (but not quite) hard and fast line of demarcation between these two elements in the population. Slaves, for the most part, were foreign. The choicest of them came from the mountains in the north, called Lulluland, and the handsomest and strongest and best slaves are specified as Lullians.

One peculiar type of slave requires special mention. They were the Habiru, characterized as being voluntary slaves. The Habiru, as they were known in the ancient Near East, were the footloose men who had only two careers open to them: they could go about marauding in bands, harrying the provinces of rulers who were unable to maintain public security; or they could enter voluntary slavery. However ridiculous "voluntary slavery" sounds to our ears, it is a fact in the ancient Near East and has an economic basis. Some people would prefer to be a slave for life in the house of a millionaire, with the guarantee of three meals a day and clothing and a roof over their heads, than to face the uncertainty of the future that poor but free men may have to face. And so we hear, in the archives of Tehiptilla alone, of many Habiru entering his household as voluntary slaves. These Habiru "contracts" appear in the other Nuzu archives as well.

Our attitude to such a matter is to me convincing disproof of the notion that our lives are determined essentially by economic considerations. Economically, no doubt, many of us would be better off if we became the permanent slaves of some plutocrat, provided he treated us right. We might even get all sorts of opportunities that would be otherwise denied to us. Yet this is so distasteful that it is unacceptable and even unthinkable to most of us. However, if economic considerations were supreme, we should gladly seize on such an opportunity as the Habiru actually did.

In Nuzu, men sold themselves into slavery in order to obtain, for instance, a wife. In other words, men who knew that they would never have enough money to pay the bride price for a wife of their own, held that it was better to be a married slave than a free bachelor. This nearly parallels the story of Jacob, who worked so long (though not technically as a slave) to win his bride from her father.

Other slaves come into slavery with their wives. The rule is that if a slave brings his own wife, their children are free-born; but if the master of the house provides the wife, the children are the master's slaves.

The laws of the land decreed that the freedom of native-born citizens was inviolable; that it could neither be wrested away from them against their will nor bartered away willingly. One would imagine that this law of the inalienability of freedom would be respected by all the people whom it was designed to protect. But nothing of the sort! People got into debt, and while the law forbade them to sell themselves as slaves, there were ways of getting around the law. For one thing, they managed it by abusing the institution of temporary exchange. For example, a man would say: For so many loads of barley, or so many measures of wool, or so many weights of precious metal, I exchange my full-time personal services. Sometimes a time limit was set to this contract, but sometimes there was no time limit, in which case it effectively circumvented the prohibition of selling one's liberty. And they not only sold their own liberty, but fathers would barter the freedom of their children, to pay off debts, or to get food, or for monetary consideration. To call such procedures "exchanges" is at best a euphemism.

A girl could not be handled in the same way, because her presence in the house of the master might be abused. But there was a way to get around this law also: She could be assigned as "a daughter and a future daughter-in-law" (or some other form of seeming "adoption") to a person who would often promise to provide her with a home and to commit himself to see that she would eventually be married to someone in, or out of, the household. On the surface there was nothing wrong with this, for every girl ought to be provided with a husband. But every girl had a monetary value (usually forty shekels of silver) as a marriage price, and so the father was really as a rule selling his daughter for about forty shekels with which to pay his debts. Sometimes he would specify that she should be married only to a free man, or that at any rate her children should be guaranteed their freedom. But often it was stated that the girl may be married off to one of the slaves in the house, and sometimes it is even stipulated that her children would be slaves also. For instance, one father makes over his daughter as "a future daughter-in-law" to Tehiptilla, and Tehiptilla specifies that she is to be married to one of his slaves; if that slave dies, to a second of his slaves; if he dies, to a third; and if he dies, to a fourth slave. In other words, even the death of three husbands will not free the girl from slavery in the household of Tehiptilla; and all the latter wanted, of course, was to have his male slaves well equipped with wives so that lots of little slaves would grow and be available for future labor, in his own old age and in the next generation of his household.

So much for one of the wise laws that human shortsightedness and greed found means to thwart. But before we move on to another topic, let us emphasize the point that not all slaves were of equal status any more than all free men are of equal status. Thus a slave named Hinzuraya was a prosperous business woman and her children were born free.

Another law was based on the sound principle that the "good earth" was the source of subsistence, and that therefore real estate must be inalienable to prevent the poor from becoming poorer, and the rich richer. It could not be sold from family to family, but, as the means of subsistence, had to be kept within the clan. But again, grasping and greedy men found a way to get around the law. The socially valid institution of adoption proved convenient for circumventing the land law. Tehiptilla, for instance, had himself adopted as the son of several hundred people in the town, and accordingly obtained the right to inherit their property. He thus became the son of many fathers; and in exchange he gave each of his fathers a "filial gift" (not, of course, a sale price, God forbid!) of so many shekels, or of donkeys, or of barley. So he kept within the law and soon snapped up vast tracts of land.

Sale adoptions can easily be differentiated from real adoptions. In real adoptions, it is specified that the adopted son is to respect the parents, and shelter and care for them for life, and bury and mourn for them when they are dead. These provisos are absent from sale adoptions. In sale adoptions the "filial gift" is clearly specified, whereas it is absent in real adoptions.

The status of women is particularly interesting in these documents. Many people labor under the misapprehension that in antiquity women were reduced to humiliating conditions, from which they have been emancipated only in modern times. But this is not in accordance with the facts. Thus, several rich and powerful women are mentioned in the Nuzu documents. One Amminae was actually the governor of a considerable province, which had been assigned to her by Saushattar, king of the Mitanni Empire. Then there was a female counterpart of Tehiptilla in the person of Tulpunnaya whom we have already mentioned. She was as successful and unscrupulous as any man in her methods of acquiring wealth. She entered into many sale adoptions, making herself the adopted daughter of many men so as to obtain their lands. Her devices were just as ruthless as those of Tehiptilla, if not more so. For instance, she acquired a girl named Shitanka as a so-called daughter and prospective daughter-in-law; and these are the marriage prospects she offered Shitanka: The latter was to be married to a slave of Tulpunnaya; if that slave died, to a second; then to a third; and so on down to a clause that if the tenth slave husband died, she was to be married to an eleventh. There was no way out for Shitanka; and it was also stipulated (and this is something strange, even in the most brutally obvious pseudo-adoptions) that Tulpunnaya had the right to hire Shitanka out as a harlot, as an alternative to marrying her off. (To be sure, prostitution did not bear the stigma it has in our society. In passing, we may note that though a girl named Eluanza was well known as a prostitute, she was nevertheless to fetch forty shekels of silver, the standard bride price for the average girl. Apparently her profession did not lower her value in the marriage market.)

Another series of documents concerns the welfare of a woman named Kizaya, another victim of Tulpunnaya, who comes to court and tells the judge that Tulpunnaya has tried to force her to marry a man named Mannuya whom she did not like, whereas she wanted to marry Arteya, whom she loved. For some reason, Tulpunnaya lost the case, and Kizaya was given leave to marry the man she wanted. Later, Kizaya tried to leave Tulpunnaya's estate, but this time Tulpunnaya was able to have her way in court, and Kizaya was forbidden to leave. Eventually, Kizaya had to turn over her son (presumably born as a free human-being to herself and Arteya) as a slave to Tulpunnaya.

Many men, as well as women, became the slaves of Tulpunnaya. One named Puhishenni "exchanged" his personal services for a shipment of barley, without specifying any time limit to the service, and we are almost sure that he remained a slave for life. Another, Arili, oddly enough exchanged himself for food and clothing during *fifty years* of service in her house; and again he could hardly have hoped to survive such a long term. (Compare our ninety-nine year leases.) So we see how men, as well as women, fell into her clutches. Other men also gave their sons over to Tulpunnaya. Two men gave her their sons in exchange for barley, one for six years' service, one for twenty years.

Tulpunnaya got into legal entanglements of one kind or another, but in the court records she was almost invariably successful in defending her cases. In one case, a man named Killi opened the locks to irrigate his field at a time when the water was due to her. She won that case, for the commissioner of irrigation testified that the water was hers and not Killi's at that point.

Before leaving the status of women it would be interesting to note that one of the most highly educated men of the town, none other than a scribe, was the slave of a lady of Nuzu. On all counts we can see that the ladies of Nuzu were not without power.

One interesting social feature of the life of Nuzu was the element of fratriarchy in society, i.e., the jurisdiction of a brother over his brothers and sisters. Some explanation of this social institution is called for especially because it has come to light only in recent years. A pure fratiarchal system would work out according to this pattern: If a man had a number of sons and died, one son (usually the oldest) would be the head of the family; but when that son died, a son of the latter would not be next in line, but instead the second brother; and so down through the line of brothers till they had all died. Then, and only then would a grandson of the original man start a new succession of brothers. In a family that had a long fratriarchal line, one brother (not necessarily the eldest) would be the official fratriarch, and a second the vice-fratriarch. It is interesting (though Biblical scholars have not generally recognized it) to see this same terminology, reflecting a similar institution, in the Old Testament, particularly in Chronicles, where "fratriarch" and "first-born" are sharply differentiated, and where vice-fratriarchs are specified.

Side by side with the fratriarchate was the less common sororarchate: the jurisdiction of a sister over her brothers and sisters. I will give one striking illustration: Shitanka, the handmaid of Tulpunnaya, actually disposed of her brother and handed him over to Tulpunnaya as a slave. It is interesting to find an account of a sister disposing of her brother in this way. More often, of course, the reverse was the case, the brother disposing of the sister.

As we come to a discussion of the institution of marriage, I wish to recall at the outset that the word "marriage" tends to be used nowadays very uncritically, as if all marriages were alike regardless of the conditions of the marriage in question. But a moment's reflection should remind us that even today a Catholic marriage is not the same as a Protestant marriage; the one rules out divorce, while in the other, divorce can often be had without too much difficulty. Or, in the Near East, when a woman marries a Moslem, unless it is specified in the marriage contract that the husband is limited to this one

wife, he is entitled to three more wives without divorc-
ing any of them. Furthermore, he may divorce any of
them without cause by saying "I divorce you" three
times in public. So marriage is not just marriage; it is
many different things according to the type of marriage
that is entered into. Easterners both in antiquity and in
modern times are more definite and intelligent about
the marriage contract than we are in the West. In the
Near East, the bride and groom state definitely what
they expect of each other, in their marriage contracts.
They do not just sign a standard form on the dotted
line. They say exactly what they are to give and take
after marriage, and they are held to it.

In the community of Nuzu there were a good many
varieties of marriages, judging by the contracts that have
been found. I shall start with the most aristocratic marriage of which we have a record in the Nuzu documents. Shilwateshup, son of the king, married his sister
Shuwarhepa to Zigi. It was specified in the marriage
contract that Zigi was never to take a second wife during her lifetime, nor to take a concubine. The sons of
the bride are to be the heirs of Zigi, and any children
that he may have by any (former?) wife are to be rele-
gated to second place. Moreover, Zigi did not apparently
pay for this bride with a bride price; she was not bartered to him as far as we can tell. This was a dignified
and aristocratic marriage in which such matters had evidently no place. It is clear that the contract is to the advantage of the bride, who was of superior social status;
and probably any children of the union would belong

to the family of the mother and not of the father. When a man paid a marriage price for his bride, he thus bought the right to the children. But in this contract, Zigi pays no price which would entitle him to the children.

The standard marriage price for the average girl, as I have remarked earlier, was forty shekels of silver. Sometimes, interestingly enough, this was paid on the installment plan. I might call attention at this juncture to the fact that in countries where a marriage price is paid, women feel very sorry for the women of America and other lands who are given away for nothing. To them that is a great humiliation. The greater a woman's price in the marriage market, the greater her pride in herself and in her relations with her husband for the rest of her life.

While women are frequently given away in marriage without their consent (and we must not forget that we still retain the ceremony of giving the bride away), according to a few of the Nuzu documents the bride is consulted, and her consent is of sufficient importance to be specified. One girl, who apparently had no parent or guardian, actually married herself off. She received from Tehiptilla ten shekels of silver and in exchange became the wife of one of his slaves.

Marriage in Nuzu seems to have been on a permanent basis, as a rule; even as it still is in that part of the world, in spite of the ease with which a man may divorce a woman. A man who has worked hard and saved enough to invest in a wife is not likely to go into the divorce courts and lose his investment. Desertions are rare in the

Nuzu documents and in each case it is the woman who deserts the man. (In such cases in the East, the woman "goes home to father," not "to mother.") In one case, Shurihil is deserted by his wife. He goes to court and gets a constable with whom he makes for her father's house. Shurihil demands the return of his wife, and her father, recognizing that he as a father has no legal claim to his married daughter, discreetly hands her over to Shurihil. Another case of desertion had more serious complications. Kushuhari had been abandoned by his wife, who had gone home to Kiripsheri, who was probably her father, but perhaps her brother. Kushuhari had a constable with him when he went to Kiripsheri's house. However, Kiripsheri violently struck the deserted husband three times, while the constable, instead of protecting him, stood by, and merely reported the incident to the court. The victim told the court that he had been struck before the very eyes of the constable, and that the constable had made no effort to protect him. We do not know whether or how Kushuhari got his wife back.

There is only one divorce case in all the 1,500 tablets that have been published. Divorce is carried out in the same calm matter-of-fact way as marriage and other transactions. The girl went back to her father, a slight monetary adjustment was made, and the matter was closed apparently without ill-will.

A husband in his will may decree that his sons are to serve their mother, while the mother is given the right to devise the estate after her death to the son, who had served her best. But a restriction is sometimes placed on the future widow: nothing was to be given to a strange man. The husband did not mind the estate going to anyone in the family, or to a favorite son; but not to a strange man. One of the oddest things is a quaint custom found in some last wills and testaments, that if the wife after the death of her husband leaves her house and marries another man, the sons shall take their mother, strip her, and drive her naked out of the house. Variations of this custom are attested in a cuneiform tablet from Hana (on the Middle Euphrates), in the Book of Hosea, in Aramaic incantations of about the sixth century A.D. in Southern Mesopotamia (see the tenth chapter); and, most strangely, in Tacitus, who reports it as a custom among the primitive Germans.

The law courts were all in all very lively places, and their records contain the greatest variety, for the situations were of course more varied than those of routine business and family affairs. In the Nuzu law courts, a man would have to prove his point by witnesses. In no tablet is there only one witness; as in the Hebrew Scriptures, a minimum of two witnesses seems to be required. If a man wishes to contradict the evidence of the other party, he is asked to take the "ordeal oath of the gods." This was evidently a nerve-racking procedure and the litigant seldom chooses to go through with it. Instead, the Nuzians preferred to concede the case to the other party. (The ordeal oath of the gods is mentioned in the Book of Exodus though the plain meaning of the Hebrew has been altered in English and other translations, on account of theological scruple.)

Another way to settle a deadlock was to send litigants to the river for a water ordeal. This again was a thing from which they usually shrank back, and they would rather abandon the case than submit to it.

Ordeals, by the by, often have a sounder basis than we imagine. Among some Bedouin Arabs it is held that if you are telling the truth in court, your tongue will not be seared by momentary contact with a red-hot spoon; but if you are guilty and lying, it will be. In practice, this is physiologically correct, for if you are not nervous, the flow of saliva will be normal and your tongue can bear the brief touch of a hot spoon; but if your tongue is dry from fear, it will be scorched.

The Nuzu courts were filled with all sorts of cases—business misunderstandings, negligence, theft, and assault and battery. But really major crimes are conspicuous by their absence. The one exception is the protracted case of the citizens of Nuzu against "His Excellency the Lord Mayor" Kushiharbe. Kushiharbe was the most prominent of all the mayors of Nuzu, and many of the tablets date from his time in office. He flourished during the days of the second, and probably greatest, generation in Nuzu; the one in which Tehiptilla lived, in the early fifteenth century B.C. "Kushiharbe" is a Cassite name, and the animosity that the citizens felt toward him may have stemmed to some extent from the fact that he was an outsider. The dossier of this case is not complete, but there are enough tablets filled with the complaints of the citizens against their mayor to show that the case was obviously a long and serious affair. The various sessions were heard before different judges, with different witnesses, on different occasions; and the amount of evidence is so telling that though the conclusion of the case has unfortunately not yet come to light, we may rest assured that the mayor was indicted, impeached, and severely punished.

I need list only a few of the specific charges against him: He was accused of stealing wood from a government project in order to do some building on his own estate. He denied the charge vehemently, but his own carpenter admitted doing the job with wood known to be government property. So the mayor had not a leg to stand on. Then another man accused him of having illicit relations with a girl, Humerelli. Again he denied the charge, but another witness came and testified to another tête-à-tête with Humerelli and this did not help Kushiharbe's case. One group of victims testified that they had given bribes to a henchman of his called Peshkillishu, who apparently served much the same function as the "gunman" of our gangsters of a decade ago. These victims had given the bribes in order to get (to pervert?) justice, and their accusation was that though he had accepted the bribe, he had not "done justice" as he had promised. Others testified that Peshkillishu had broken their doors and rifled their houses; others, that he had impressed seals illegally in order to convert their property to Kushiharbe. A long list of people accused the mayor and his strong-armed henchmen of robbery aggravated by beatings or illegal imprisonment, or threats of such abuse. One man reports his brother had been taken away and held till ransomed. Another relates that his wife had been kidnaped and held for ransom. Still another had been robbed of his sheep while his daughter-in-law was taken away and held for eleven months. Robbing men of their cattle was a common occurrence, and many testified to this charge against Kushiharbe and Peshkillishu. The latter was also accused of entering and stripping several houses. The witnesses would come along one after another; as many as a dozen of them in a tablet; each pressing a serious charge against the mayor and his "thugs." One man pitifully complained that one of the latter, Ziliptilla, had seized a ram of his, slaughtered it, and sat down to a meal of mutton. There was one especially circumstantial complaint: Peshkillishu had kidnaped a man and held him for ransom. After two months, the victim's family thought they would try to rescue him, so one brother got a guide from the capital, Arrap-ha, and paid him to take him to the place where his brother was being held. On the way back the rescuing brother was murdered and the guide kidnaped; and then the guide's father collected damages from the original victim's family in whose service his son had been kidnaped.

Another mayor was implicated in the course of the trial and there is a good possibility that the mayors had an organized intercity crime racket. But it is interesting to find that these ancient communities were not subject to absolute dictatorship and could free themselves from tyranny by due process of law without resorting to open rebellion. They were able to bring their highest municipal officials to trial, to expose even the mayor's crimes and apparently to have him expelled from office and punished. In passing we may note how well Kushiharbe's trial brings out the usefulness of an independent judiciary.

One of the most surprising results of a study of the Nuzu tablets is the light they shed on the Patriarchal Age of the Old Testament: the period of Abraham, Isaac, and Jacob. As we know, the social institutions at that age were not the same as they were among the later Israelites; for the laws that governed Abraham, Isaac, and Jacob were not the same as the laws set down in the later "Mosaic" law. What is surprising is that many of the peculiar social institutions of the patriarchal period are also characteristic of the Nuzu community. This is in itself a large subject, and I shall give only a few illustrations here. We recall that Abraham and Sarah were childless for a long time and that Eliezar, a slave, was made heir apparent of Abraham. It was normal, as we have seen in the Nuzu documents, for a childless couple to adopt a son (even from the slave class) to look after them. But in the Nuzu documents it was specified that if later a real child should be born to that couple, he should be the heir, and not the adopted son. And in Scripture, God assured Abraham that Eliezar would not inherit him but that he would beget a real son as an heir. Eventually Isaac was born and so Eliezar naturally yielded to him the right to inherit.

Sarah, childless as she was, gave her handmaid Hagar to her husband, and interpreters have assumed she did that out of the goodness of her heart, but that was not the case. It was regularly stipulated in the marriage contracts of Nuzu that if a wife did not produce a child for her husband she was to supply him with a handmaid who would, for the purpose of marriage was not companionship but the procreation of an heir to carry on the family line and the integrity of the home. It was also stipulated in the Nuzu documents that the wife was not allowed to drive out the offspring of the handmaid. Sarah did, of course, drive out Hagar and her son Ishmael; but it was necessary for God to give Abraham a special dispensation to allow this; so the thing must have been normally illegal, as in the Nuzu tablets.

Another strange feature of the Patriarchal Age is the selling of the birthright. We know that Esau, in exchange for a mess of lentils, sold his birthright to his grasping brother Jacob. There is a direct parallel to this in one of the tablets dealing with a "horrid" Nuzu family. Kurpazah, the son of Hilbishuh, got a grove belonging to his brother Tupkitilla in exchange for three sheep. Obviously when a man exchanges a fertile grove, which is probably to be one of his chief means of subsistence, and perhaps his only inheritance portion, it means only one thing: that it was dictated by dire necessity; specifically, to avert starvation. We know that Jacob took advantage of Esau in a similar situation.

The family of Hilbishuh appears over and over in the annals of Nuzu, in the second worst series of scandals of this town. A number of characters figure in them, and as we read them we feel like some old gossip who has lived in a small town for eighty years and knows all the doings and misdoings of the other residents.

In another case, Kurpazah committed assault and battery on the wife of his brother, Matteshup. In still another court record, Matteshup testified that he saw his brother Kurpazah stealing sheep from the estate of still another brother, Tupkitilla. So we see that the accuser, the culprit, and the informer, are all brothers: the shameful sons of Hilbishuh.

Before closing this discussion we might well observe that the relations between Laban and Jacob are particularly replete with Nuzu parallels. We shall mention only the most striking of many points: that curious episode of Rachel's stealing her father's household gods. This has puzzled commentators greatly, but we now know from the Nuzu documents that the possession of the household gods was tantamount to the title to an estate. Rachel stole them not so much for religious reasons but to secure the estate of her father for her husband and their children, rather than for her brothers, one of whom would normally have become the chief heir.

CHAPTER IX

MILITARY CORRESPONDENCE FROM THE LAST DAYS OF JUDAH

THERE ARE certain handicaps in dealing with subjects that touch on the Bible, because people tend to take either an overconservative or an overradical attitude in such matters. I am often asked whether archaeological discoveries have "proved" the Bible, or "disproved" the Bible. The fact is, that archaeological discoveries are not supposed either to prove or disprove Scripture. However, archaeological discoveries, coming from the world in which the Scriptures were written, indisputably add to the sum total of our knowledge of that world and give us perspective as well as more individual facts.

Most of the inscriptions bearing on Biblical times have come not from Palestine but from other parts of the Near East, especially Mesopotamia and Egypt. Palestine itself has yielded relatively few texts from remote antiquity.

At the outset, we must evaluate briefly the Old Testament as a historical document: The Old Testament is essentially a pro-Judean and anti-Israelite book, representing the point of view of the Southern Kingdom as against that of the Northern. In the Bible every single king of Israel is a wicked king, causing the people to err, and, often enough, worse than his fathers before him. The kings of Judah, to be sure, are not all made out to be saints; they are represented sometimes as good and sometimes bad; but the kings of Israel, as portrayed in the Old Testament, are quite beyond redemption.

We can go still further with regard to the Old Testament, and say that it is not only pro-Judean but specifically pro-Jerusalemite; with now a lack of consideration, and now a disregard for, the provinces. This is more or less the necessary result of the fact that the government as well as the religious cult, were centralized at Jerusalem, and any decentralization, religiously as well as politically, would be looked upon askance by the Jerusalem party. For this reason, the Biblical evidence for the Judean provinces is biased and sketchy.

One of the great mounds southwest of Jerusalem is Tell ed Duweir. Many scholars think that this is the location of the ancient city of Lachish, and I am inclined to accept the identification, though it is still open to some doubt. We know that there were *two* great cities in that district, Lachish and Azeqa; both are mentioned in the texts discussed in this chapter.

Tell ed Duweir is an imposing mound. It attracted the attention of the late Mr. J. L. Starkey, who was in my opinion the finest technician in Palestinian field archaeology. His excavations were models of neatness, and deserved the fine results that they yielded. Starkey at Tell ed Duweir found the most important collection of Hebrew inscriptions ever discovered. All his colleagues regretted his unfortunate death on January 10, 1938, when he disregarded the advice of his colleagues and fearlessly attempted to motor to Jerusalem. Palestine was then in a chaotic condition and he was murdered by Arabs en route.

The Duweir texts are ostraca. An ostracon is a piece of pottery inscribed with ink. Unfortunately, inscriptions on parchment and on papyrus normally decay with the years in the moist soil of Palestine. Indeed, such materials have been preserved extensively only in Egypt, where the dryness of the soil keeps organic matter from decomposing. Luckily stone and ostraca are spared regardless of climate.

Most of the Duweir ostraca are letters; the only letters that have come down to us from the ancient Hebrew people.

We might note that the two oldest known extensive manuscripts of the Hebrew Bible date from 895 and 916 A.D., respectively, so that even the best available manuscripts of Scripture are copies of copies of copies, and some corruptions have certainly crept in. In my opinion, the corruptions are surprisingly few, but the manuscripts cannot possibly be just as they were when first written. The inscriptions on our ostraca, however, have come to us unchanged (save where the ink has faded); and therefore, as such are more authentic word for word, and letter for letter, than our manuscripts of the Bible. But do not misunderstand me; I am not saying that this group of letters from an ancient mound in Palestine is of greater value historically than the Bible;

far from it. The Scriptures are a mine of source material, where the ostraca are but a drop in the bucket compared with all we know of the Hebrew people from the Bible. But what little is in the ostraca is textually more authentic, all things being equal.

The ostraca reflect one of the great moments in human history. Palestine was one of the little buffer states between the Babylonian and Egyptian empires. The Neo-Babylonian empire under Nebuchadnezzar had grown from strength to strength and was engulfing everything. The Egyptian empire had long been decadent. The Judean king was a vassal of Nebuchadnezzar. Unfortunately, the defiant spirit of independence, characteristic of the ancient Hebrew people, challenged the authority of the great Nebuchadnezzar, and such a course could only lead to their military defeat. In 597 B.C. Nebuchadnezzar made his first onslaught against Judah, reduced the country, and took captive the king, who was only eighteen years old. The latter is known to us under two Hebrew names: Konyahu, or Yehoyakin. He was carried off to Babylon; but for the Jewish people he was the legitimate successor of the house of David; and accordingly, in the opening chapter of the New Testament, the ancestry of Jesus is traced through him and not through Zedekiah, the last king who ruled at Jerusalem.

The country was greatly impoverished by the first Babylonian captivity (in 597 B.C.) not so much by the things as by the human beings that were taken away. Nebuchadnezzar's policy was to deplete a subjected land of its aristocrats, its craftsmen, its leaders, and the whole uppercrust of the population, leaving only the poorest behind.

Mattanyahu, a close kinsman of Konyahu, was selected by Nebuchadnezzar and placed upon the throne of Judah. Mattanyahu is generally known by the name Nebuchadnezzar gave him on that occasion; to wit, Zedekiah. He swore allegiance as a vassal to Nebuchadnezzar, and he remained loyal until he was induced by the independence party to revolt. Doubtless he was encouraged in this also by Egyptian propagandists and others who wished to break the grip Nebuchadnezzar had on Western Asia.

In the ninth year of the reign of Zedekiah, Nebuchadnezzar came against the cities of Judah, and before long all but three of the fortified cities—the capital, Jerusalem, and Azeqa and Lachish to the southwest, were in the hands of the Babylonians.

Most of what we know of this period is found recorded in the Book of Jeremiah, who was the great personality during the last days of Judah. He started out as a member of a priestly family in the little village of Anathoth, north of Jerusalem, but he abandoned his priestly calling and his home and went to the capital, where he felt his message should be delivered. Like all the prophets, he was essentially interested in establishing justice within the matrix of Yahwism. His policy was that of loyalty to Babylon; at least he considered it foolish to resist Nebuchadnezzar. He was definitely anti-Egyptian. His book is full of exquisite poetry as well as of prose accounts of historic events; but what is important for us to note is that it tells essentially of happenings in Jerusalem; necessarily so for the final period when the capital was cut off by the two-year siege by the Babylonians. So for a first-hand glimpse into what was happening in the provinces in those critical days, we turn to the new inscriptions.

The texts reflect a tragic situation; a little people fighting against all odds and whose chief arms were courage and faith in God. The characters mentioned are not those of the Biblical account. The army men and prophets of our ostraca would be unsung and forgotten if it were not for the texts, eighteen of which came to light in 1935, and three more in 1938.

Unfortunately, only the first four of the twenty-one texts can be translated with more or less completeness. The difficulty in interpreting even the unbroken ostraca arises from two facts: one, that the ink is faded, so that it is exceedingly hard to establish with certainty the identity of many (alphabetic) letters—though the forms of all the letters of the alphabet are known; the other, that the style is very terse: the writers will mention one topic in one brief sentence and then change the subject in the next short sentence. The style is, so to speak, telegraphic. The correspondents understood the letters without trouble, since they were keeping in constant touch with one another; while *we* can only guess at what is reflected in this correspondence between the ancient leaders of the southern forces of Judah. We await further progress in deciphering the ostraca, but any advance made in this field is not likely to result from the study of printed texts or articles on the subject. The one reliable source available to every scholar is the photographs published in an English edition and in the less sumptuous (but later and complete) Hebrew edition. All the additional equipment the scholar needs is a pair of good eyes, a magnifying glass, a knowledge of Hebrew idiom and palaeography, and, above all, common sense. The growing results of many scholars' labors are steadily extracting the history enshrined in the ostraca.

In the two preceding chapters, we have dealt with great groups of texts, whose rich contents we have had to summarize. But here the material itself is so limited in quantity that we can deal with the complete texts, one after the other, provided that the necessary background is supplied as we go along.

In the first document there is no account of any action. It is merely a list of five men, named, in accordance with Hebrew custom, after the pattern: X the son of Y. Virtually all of the names end in -*yahu*, the form that "Yahweh" takes when used at the end of personal names (as is characteristic of the personal names in the Bible during this period). This is interesting because it reflects the fact that the Hebrews during the generation that preceded the destruction of the First Temple in 586, were not guilty of apostasy; for the written records clearly show them naming their children after Yahweh. One must remember that this was not always so, and in some early periods things were quite different. Thus, a grandson of King Saul, for instance, was named Meribaal, after Baal. So undivided devotion to Yahweh was not characteristic of the Hebrews throughout all their history. Some of the characters in "Ostracon 1" have the same names as certain Old Testament characters, but they are not to be identified with them any more than one "John Smith" need to be the same as another of the same name. Here is the text, which may well have been used as a sort of roll call:

> *Gemaryahu son of Hissilyahu*
> *Yaäzanyahu son of Tovshillem*
> *Hagab son of Yaäzanyahu*
> *Mivtahyahu son of Yirmiyahu*
> *Mattanyahu son of Neriyahu.*

Yirmiyahu is normally Anglicized as Jeremiah, the same as the name of the prophet. Mattanyahu was the name of Zedekiah before he was appointed king by Nebuchadnezzar. And Neriyahu is none other than the name of the father of Jeremiah's scribe, Baruch. Yaäzanyahu occurs in the English Bible as "Jaazaniah" and on a seal found in the excavations at Tell en Nasba, north of Jerusalem; all from the same age. In other words, the names fit in perfectly with other names known to us from this period of Bible history.

The second document is a letter. According to the etiquette of the Hebrew language, you should normally address your superior not in the second but in the third person: not "thou," but "my lord"; while you refer to yourself also in the third person: not "I," but "thy slave" or "his slave." Furthermore, though this may sound odd to Occidental ears, you may refer to yourself as a dog: "thy slave, a (or thy) dog." This occurs not only in the Hebrew Scriptures, but also in the Amarna letters from Canaan.

This first letter starts with the equivalent of an "address": "To my lord—." The person addressed is Yaüsh, who is apparently commander-in-chief of the forces in the district of Lachish and Azeqa. He was probably an able leader and evidently put up a brave fight, while keeping in constant touch with his men. Following the "address" comes the greeting, which is a new one in literature and is so pleasing that some of the teachers of modern Hebrew in Palestine are trying to reintroduce it into the colloquial and written language. It occurs in variant form thus: "May Yahweh cause my lord to hear tidings of good" or "tidings of peace," or "to see tidings of peace." The body of the letter is introduced with the phrase "Now at present; now at present," which might be rendered in colloquial English: "Now to get down to business."

This epistle may well contain tragic news, informing the commander-in-chief of the military defeat under the captain who writes this letter. The writer also acknowledges the receipt of a letter which the general Yaüsh had sent him some time before. This is a literal translation of Ostracon No. 2:

To my lord, Yaüsh. May Yahweh cause my lord to hear tidings of peace! Now at present; now at present: Who is thy slave, a dog, that my lord hath remembered his slave? May Yahweh remember our (?) defeat (?) of which thou dost not know!

In the third inscription, an officer, Hoshayahu, is writing to his superior, doubtless the same Yaüsh; for all the texts but one were found together and probably form a single file of correspondence sent to the commander-in-chief. In this letter the writer refers to a letter he had received the day before, and is upset about a misunderstanding alluded to in it. He has been scolded for not reading or not heeding a letter, and he explains that he never received it and so could not read it; he protests his innocence and swears by Yahweh. I should perhaps call attention to the fact that the commandment "Thou shalt not take the name of the Lord thy God in vain" is generally misunderstood, and does not mean what the English translation conveys to Anglo-Saxon ears. It should be translated: "Do not swear to a falsehood by the name of Yahweh, thy God." Jeremiah, for instance, tells the people they should swear more (not less) by Yahweh, but stop swearing by other gods. Thus the Bible teaches that it is sinful either to swear anything by a false god, or to swear falsely by the true God. The ostraca give us no grounds for suspecting the Judean leaders of swearing by Baal or other pagan gods, or of turning away from the true God. All swearing in official circles is definitely by Yahweh, the national God of Judah. After protesting his innocence and swearing it by Yahweh, Hoshayahu reports various news items to his superior. Thus a "captain of the host" named Konyahu (?), had gone down to

Egypt, taking with him Hodoyahu and his men from the place where this letter was written. The Book of Jeremiah refers to campaigns to Egypt either for help or for supplies, and this was natural, for if the Judeans were fleeing from the Babylonians, there was no other place of escape, and if they wanted to get food, there was no other place to procure it. This, then, quite reflects the conditions as we know them from Scripture. Hoshayahu reports also that he had forwarded a letter of warning from Toviyahu, "the slave of the king," that had been delivered to a man named Shallum by a prophet. This prophet was not necessarily, nor even probably, Jeremiah himself, for there were a number of prophets active at the time; he was perhaps a prophet with essentially the same message as Jeremiah, but who left no book behind him. The warning of the prophet (?) may have been just one of exhortation to his fellow Judeans to be faithful to Yahweh. "The slave of the king" is a high title, designating not a slave, but a kind of minister of state. "The king" can be none other than Zedekiah, though he is never mentioned by name; in these texts he is always referred to by title alone.

This is text No. 3, the most extensive and circumstantial letter of the collection:

Thy servant Hoshayahu is sending to tell my lord Yaüsh: May Yahweh cause my lord to hear tidings of peace! Now at present; now at present: I have indeed opened (?) my eyes at the letter my lord sent thy slave yesterday. For the heart of thy slave hath been sick since thou didst send unto thy slave. And when my lord saith: Canst thou not read a letter? by Yahweh, nobody ever attempted to read me a letter, nor have I read any letter that came to me! . . . I deposited it . . . (a letter?; the writing is faint and the context unclear). *And it hath been related to thy slave saying: The captain of the host, Konyahu (?), son of Eltnatan, went down to enter Egypt and sent to take Hodoyahu, son of Ahiyahu, and his men from here. And as for the letter of Toviyahu, the slave of the king, which came to Shallum from the prophet saying: Be on thy guard! thy slave hath sent it to my lord.*

The fourth ostracon informs the superior that the sender has followed all the superior's orders and written them "on the door." It is not likely that many Judeans, military or civilian, could read; but this was apparently the normal way to publicize a document. The door served as a bulletin board, and once a document had been so posted, it would be the business of the officers and possibly others to find out what the notice was.

The writer informs his superior officer (in all probability Yaüsh) that the town of Beth ha Rafa (?) has been deserted. The superior has also been inquiring as to the whereabouts of a certain Semakyahu, whom the writer reports has been taken and brought up to "the city," which scholars are inclined to identify with Jerusalem, though we cannot be certain of this point. He suggests that the superior give specific instructions that he may go and fetch Semakyahu, who must be in the vicinity of the city. He assures his general that he has been looking for all the Lachish signals. It is interesting to note that they had some sort of conventional means of signaling: whether by fire, or by waving sticks in keeping with a kind of semaphore system, or by some other way, we do not yet know with certainty, but the Mishna is probably right in defining the term as a fire signal. What is certain is that the captains kept in touch with each other through a forerunner of telegraphy and reported in writing regularly to headquarters as to whether the signals were being sighted. At the end of the present letter, the writer tragically remarks that while they are observing the signals of Lachish they cannot see the signals of Azeqa. This very likely means that Azeqa had already fallen into the hands of the Babylonian invaders. In laconic style, our writer thus records the fall of one of the three remaining cities. It is to be noted incidentally that the letter must have been written in the field, for the two cities in the district are referred to as places from which the signals are being, or should be, sighted. This is Text 4:

May Yahweh cause my lord to hear tidings of goodness! And now, in accordance with all my lord hath sent, thus hath thy servant done. I have written on the door in accordance with all that my lord hath sent. And when my lord sendeth concerning Beth ha Rafa (?) (I herewith report that) nobody is there. And as for Semakyahu, Shemayahu hath taken him and brought him up to the city; and let my lord send thy servant thither!

Where can he be except in its vicinity? Investigate (and my lord) will know that we are watching for the signals of Lachish in accordance with all the signs that my lord hath given for the signal of Azeqa hath not been sighted.

The rest of the texts are unfortunately fragmentary, and it would be foolhardy to attempt a reconstruction of them here. For present purposes we may review the few clear passages and other interesting snatches.

In Ostracon No. 5, the writer says to his superior: "Thy slave hath returned the letters to my lord through ——yahu." And at the end of the letter, the writer is either expressing modesty or defending himself against some accusation when he exclaims: "How could thy slave help or hurt the king?", which might be paraphrased, "Who am I, to do damage or to render assistance to Zedekiah?"

The following can be made out in No. 6:

To my lord Yaüsh: May Yahweh cause my lord to see this present signal. Peace! Who is thy slave, a dog, that my lord hath sent him the letters of the captain(s). Read, I pray, and behold the words of the . . . are not good (for they are) to discourage the (people) . . . as Yahweh, thy God, liveth . . .

The oath at the end is probably in support of the writer's innocence. The "discouragement" may refer to the communication of some leader or agitator. Jeremiah, himself, was more than once accused of "discouraging the people," or, to render the Hebrew literally, "causing the hands of the people to drop." It is true that he recommended surrender but we must give him the benefit of the doubt and interpret his advice as being intended for the welfare of the people and not to betray them.

In Ostracon No. 16 there is another reference to a prophet, but he need not be the same as any mentioned in the other letters. It is very likely that in those times many prophets were in demand, to give the people the courage required by the agonizing crisis.

Text 20 is the only dated text. It begins "In the ninth year"; that is, the fateful year in which Nebuchadnezzar invaded Palestine because of Zedekiah's revolt. All but one of the letters from Tell ed Duweir may well date between that year and the fall of Lachish which preceded the destruction of Jerusalem in 587-586 B.C. (One text was found under the floor datable to Zedekiah and may therefore be assigned to 598 B.C. or earlier.)

After two years of siege the wall of Jerusalem was breached by the engines of Nebuchadnezzar, and for this we are given an exact date: the ninth day of the fourth month of the eleventh year of Zedekiah, king of Judah. The king and some of his followers made their escape, but they did not get far. They were apprehended, and Zedekiah was brought to trial. After his sons were slain in his presence, his eyes were put out and he was taken in chains to Babylon to spend the rest of his life in darkness. The land was depleted of most of its best people for a second time but Jeremiah was spared. Nebuchadnezzar had heard of his career and his policy, and perhaps he respected him also as a man of God. Jeremiah, however, though favored by the conqueror and given his freedom, was hated by most of his co-religionists. Against his protests a group of them compelled him to accompany them to the Egypt that he loathed and it was there that he probably died.

The ostraca reflect a lost battle. However, the significance of those events is not to be judged in military terms, because it was the Exile itself that tore the Jews away from their land and thus forced upon them the historically momentous decision: either to conceive of their God as the universal God, or to give up any pretense that they were still under His protection in a foreign land. Up to that time, the general concept of Yahweh had been that of a national god having jurisdiction primarily over His own tiny country. But now the Jews accepted once and for all the idea that Yahweh was the only God and that His dominion was unbounded by time and space. Thus was the way paved for later Judaism, Christianity, and Islam.

Jeremiah, in spite of his mournful "Jeremiads," expresses the constant hope of the return from exile and of the restoration of the Temple. That hope was fulfilled within the memory of some living men, when Cyrus of Persia permitted those of the exiles that wished, to return and to rebuild their temple in Zion.

The importance of the subject may justify the repetition of a few banal words before we close this chapter.

It was the message of the prophets which set the standard of morals for the Western world down to the present. And the Yahweh by whom Yaüsh and his captains swear has become the God worshiped alike in Christendom and Islam.

CHAPTER X

A WORLD OF DEMONS
AND LILITHS

IT IS MY impression that the social sciences often suffer from the fact that many scholars tend to stress the rational to the virtual exclusion of the irrational. The subject of this chapter is an irrational but real factor in human history.

Science as well as magic both stem from the desire to solve life's problems. The basic problems such as the maintenance of health, the attainment of material prosperity and security, and personal happiness, have occasioned both science and superstition. It is perhaps worthwhile here to make a fundamental distinction between science and superstition. If something appears plausible at a certain time, it may fairly be classified as scientific; but if it is later disproved and yet people adhere to it, it is then superstition. Thus to look down upon the ancient scientists of Babylonia because they believed in astrology, would be to lack historical perspective. But when a person in this day and age still adheres to the system of Sumero-Babylonian astrology, that is superstition. The number of people who still take astrology seriously in this country is nothing short of alarming. I

recently counted seven astrological journals on one news-
stand. Astrology nets millions of dollars for quacks every
year in the United States. Palmistry, phrenology, crystal-
gazing and the like are also paying propositions.

We should also make a basic distinction between science and magic. While science reckons with cause and
effect, magic disregards causality. It is often held, but
quite falsely, that savages prefer magic to science. Savages emphatically prefer science. For instance, once they
learn the principles of irrigation, they stop depending
on rituals for rain, because they can see that science
regularly brings about the calculated effect, whereas
magic obviously cannot be counted on to yield regularly
the same results as science.

For the study of magic, as for all sociological studies,
there are two main sources: living men and dead records.
To work with living men is always preferable. The records of the dead are the best sources we have for past
history, but they are relatively defective. When you observe living people practicing magic you see the magician's act (or praxis) as well as hear his words (or incantation). When you have only the written incantation the
accompanying act can as a rule only be partially sur-
mised from the words.

Incantations may be divided into two kinds: words
that have meaning in themselves (words as they are ordinarily used in conversation) and sounds (or letters or
even scrawling) that are normally meaningless (nonsense syllables). This nonsense element in magic is to
some extent common to all peoples. We find traces of

it in our folklore: e.g., "eeny-meeny-miny-mo," "Abra-cadabra," "Hocus pocus (dominocus)," and so forth. Some of these go back to meaningful speech, but they have long degenerated into the meaningless. As children, we fall heir to many vestiges of magic lore that we tend to relinquish as we grow up.

For ten years I have been collecting a group of incantation texts in the museums of Asia, Europe, and America. They come from Babylonia and are couched in a variety of Aramaic dialects. It is surprising that the general public does not know that Christ's life was conducted through the medium of Aramaic, except for some Greek that he may have used with merchants, or the Hebrew quotations that he used in the synagogue or with the learned men of his people. The fact is that Aramaic is one of the landmarks in the linguistic history of the world. At the time of the great Achaemenian Empire (from the sixth century B.C.) it was the interprovincial language of the Empire, which at its height extended from India to Ethiopia. At the time of the Alexandrian conquest the two great languages were Greek and Aramaic; and Aramaic was not displaced until Arabic spread with the rise of Islam in and after the seventh century A.D.

The first Aramaic incantation comes from Uruk. It is a unique document being the only known Aramaic text written in cuneiform characters on clay. It is just as curious as if one were to find an English document written in the hieroglyphs of Egypt.

However, the texts under discussion come from

The Aramaic incantation in cuneiform from Uruk. *Courtesy of the Louvre.* OBVERSE

The Aramaic incantation in cuneiform from Uruk. *Courtesy of the Louvre.*

Sasanian Babylonia before and after 600 A.D. These inscriptions are written spirally on terra-cotta bowls; usually on the inside of the bowl, sometimes on the outside, and sometimes on both sides. Some scholars have advanced the theory that these bowls with their inscriptions were intended as traps for demons: the demon being forced into the bowl by the incantation, whereupon the bowl is turned upside down and buried, thus trapping the demon in the ground. But this is based on false interpretations of the texts. The fact is that the last thing the ancients wished to do was to trap on their own property the demons which might subsequently escape and work mischief on the spot. The bowls are calculated to do the exact opposite: namely, to exorcise and get rid of them. While I therefore reject the aforementioned theory, I am not sure as to why the inscriptions were written on bowls. I have a theory, which I give as such for what it may be worth. A few skulls inscribed with incantations have been found from the same time and place. It is well known that a mass of superstitions and magical beliefs have always clustered around the dead and their skeletons, particularly their skulls; and these bowls, somewhat resembling the shape of the cranium, may have substituted the skulls that had been in use earlier.

As I have pointed out, the main purpose of magic is to protect the human beings who resort to it. The beginning of one of these charms expresses the purpose clearly: "This charm is designed for the health, guarding and sealing of the house (of the client)."

The people who practiced this magic were professional magicians who took the place of the physicians and scientists of our communities. To be hired as a magician, the practitioner has to have clients who believe he has magic powers. We sometimes find a magician professing his potency and magical ability in these words: "I go in (magical) strength," whereupon he lists his magical equipment. The magician may express his confidence in his own magic by such a declaration as the following: "I seize what I seek and what I ask for with the tongue I take."

As for the clients: The most curious thing is that in the incantations they are never called "So-and-so the son of such-and-such a father" as in daily life, but "So-and-so the son of such-and-such a mother." The reason is that magic must be exact, and since one can never be perfectly certain of his father, genealogy through the mother is indicated. This is not due merely to a lack of faith in female fidelity. The trouble is that demons have the habit of impersonating husbands, so that a woman may be deceived unwittingly. Consequently, we find persons desiring magical protection from male demons and female liliths "appearing to the sons of men; to men in the form of women and to women in the form of men; lying with sons of men by night and by day." This explains other peculiarities of life. For instance, if a child is downright naughty he has probably been sired by a demon. And if a child hates his father, he is not really the son of his presumable father, but of an impersonating demon. The notion that human beings and demons are constantly being hybridized explains in a charming, if not scientific, way most of life's difficulties. This makes human nature at its worst explicable. For if we were all descended purely from Adam and Eve, who were made in the image of God, we ought to be better people than we are.

One of the features about magic is its precision, albeit misguided precision. For instance, one text informs us that the magician is writing this incantation "on this day of all days, this month of all months, this year of all years, and this time of all times." There are thus auspicious occasions and propitious times for effective magic.

All the carefulness that we now find in our judicial documents is found in these magical texts. The repetition that is common in them has a legalistic ring, and it is to make sure that everything is taken care of and nothing forgotten. Note the careful listing of the items to be protected in one of the incantation bowls:

Let there be health from the heavens, and sealing and guarding unto the dwelling, threshold, residence and house and threshold of this Farukdad son of Zbinta and Qamoy daughter of Zarq and everything that they have, that this Farukdad son of Zbinta and this Qamoy daughter of Zarq may be preserved: they, their sons, daughters, oxen, asses, slaves, handmaids, all cattle great and small, that there are in this dwelling and threshold or may come to be therein,—that there may be annulled from this dwelling and threshold of this Farukdad son of Zbinta and Qamoy daughter of Zarq, Aramaean spells, Jewish spells, Arabic spells, Persian spells, Mandaean spells, Greek spells, spells of the Romans; spells that are worked in the seventy languages either by women or men.

Note too that lists such as this enumerate the possessions that these people owned: the sort of cattle they had, the sort of households, with male and female slaves, and so on. Even more interesting, this incantation gives a detailed picture of the linguistic and ethnic elements of the community: "Aramaean spells" refer to the incantations of which these inscriptions form part. There were three Aramaic dialects: Rabbinical Aramaic, Christian Aramaic (=Syriac) and Pagan Aramaic (=Mandaean). Large settlements of Jews had been in Babylonia since the days of Nebuchadnezzar and quite a few are still there. The Arabs were eventually to become the dominant element they are today. Some of the texts that have been found we suspect are Persian, but they have not yet been deciphered. However, many of the clients have good Persian names. The Mandaeans are the people sometimes called "St.-John-the-Baptist Christians." They still survive as a small sect in Iraq and Iran and are famous now for their metal work. Like many of the oriental Jews, Christians, and Moslems, the Mandaeans still practice magic on a wide scale. As for the mention of Greek and Roman elements in the community, we will recall Mesopotamia formed part of Alexander's Empire and of his Seleucid successors. It was later the frontier of the great Byzantine (or Eastern Roman) Empire. The list also

This photograph of an Aramaic bowl was made with a special lens so that the incantation on the concave surface appears without distortion. *Courtesy of the British Museum.*

An aerial view of Nuzu. Air photography is an important archaeological aid. This picture illustrates how an aerial view provides an excellent record of the completed excavation. Air photography is also a great help in exploration, revealing mounds including many features that would be missed from a ground survey.

reproduces the belief that the languages of the world are seventy in number—actually a great underestimate.

The Babylonian community was, then as always, highly mixed, linguistically and ethnically; and we shall soon see that it was also conglomerate in religion, as the magic clearly reflects. There is a less detailed summary of the people in another incantation, which specifies: "Spells of the west and east, spells of the north and south, spells of the 127 provinces." The "127 provinces" refer obviously to the empire of 127 provinces of the Achaemenian Xerxes, called Ahasuerus in the Book of Esther. This is therefore a purely historical reminiscence that survived in magical formulae. We cannot assume that such formulae must refer to contemporary conditions; they may refer to much earlier periods. Magic is quite conservative, as a rule.

A characteristic of human beings in all ages is that they people the world with all sorts of terrors, as if things were not bad enough already. For instance, as if there were not enough murders today, we must have detective stories and crime magazines and even radio thrillers for children. Mankind seems eager to scare itself out of its wits, and it often succeeds. Let me tell of some of the creatures that the inhabitants of Sasanian Babylonia manufactured to frighten themselves with: there was "the Mighty Destroyer that kills a man from beside his wife and a woman from beside her husband, and sons and daughters from their father and mother by day and by night"; there was the demon "whose height is 170 cubits and who sits under roof spouts and kills children."

Of course there were also vampires "that eat of their (victims') flesh until they are full and drink of their blood until they are sated."

It is interesting too that demons tend to be specialized, and this has a bearing on the history of science, especially the science of medicine. For instance, there is a special demon responsible for eye infections of a certain type. He is "the evil spirit that sits on the brain and causes the eye to tear." If you have migraine or other types of headache, still other demons are responsible. For each disease there is a separate demon; and interestingly enough these demons get into the victim from without: a belief that may well have paved the way for the germ theory, which is essentially the same thing, a specialized host that enters the victim from the outside. We also find the forerunner of the principle of immunization, in the helpful spirits that are used to counteract these demons: the antibodies, as it were, of the demonic world. Of course, the magicians who wrote the Aramaic bowls went far beyond the point justified by science as we know it. For instance, they held that a tremor on one side of the body was caused by a different demon from a tremor on the other side. When a man felt troubled, it was due to the demon "that strangles the thoughts of the heart." Similarly with all other evils, from dumbness to psychopathic loquacity, each was caused by a special demon.

One feature of the magic was that undesirable things were personified and given demonic status. To the Near East mentality, the word itself has a power that is greatly feared. Since the Near Easterners are given to cursing on the slightest provocation, the power of their words is a serious matter. For even though they may not mean it, they believe that the fact that they have uttered the curse can harm the person cursed.

Sometimes the demons were personified to the point where a figure of the demon is drawn on the bowl. One bowl adds the explanation: "This is the figure of the curse and lilith."

Another evil force is what Oriental and other people call "the evil eye," or, more exactly, "the evil and envious eye." The fact that some people envy other people, or begrudge them the good things of life, is supposed to bring calamity upon the envied. To this day in the Near East you should never admire a baby, or remark that a child is pretty, for such admiration would be suspected as a form of casting the evil and envious eye, causing the curse of the evil eye to afflict the child. This concept is common in many parts of the world, but it is particularly prominent in the East.

Another demon is one for which we have no good word in English, but which the Germans call "*Poltergeist.*" This is a demon that causes people to shake. I remember that when I was in Baltimore in 1938, that part of the country was agog over the case of a girl six or seven years of age, who had a *Poltergeist* that shook not only her body but the bed she lay on. Oddly enough, *Poltergeists* are generally found in connection with children, and especially with little girls. Most are cases of exhibitionism whereby children wanting to attract attention get it by such spectacular means.

These texts specify many curses of relatives, particularly of female relatives. For instance, according to one incantation the client wishes to be protected "from the curse, invocation, knock, evil eye, wicked sorceries, sorceries of mother and daughter, daughter-in-law and mother-in-law, and of the presumptuous woman who makes the eyes go black and who blows away the soul."

Another text summarizes the evil forces as follows: "from the angels of destruction, from all the evil sorceries and mighty practices—from all spirits, devils, demons, lilis (the male counterparts of liliths), idols, strokes, curses, invocations, the curse, witchcraft, the evil and envious eye, and everything bad." Note that the end of the formula is intended to guarantee completeness.

Demons do not always look demonic. They may take rather innocent and deceptive forms. For this reason, the wary client wishes to be protected also from disguised evil spirits, such as those "that appear in the form of vermin or reptiles, in the form of beast or bird, and in the form of man or woman, and in any form or species." Again, note the all-embracing end of the formula.

Curses and vows are also classified according to the authority giving them power, such as the deity sanctioning the magic. One client thus wishes to be immune from the curses "which they have sworn and performed by the gods of the heaven and the gods of the earth;

they have sworn by male gods and female goddesses."
This classification goes back to the old pagan inhabitants who lived there in the early third millennium B.C.,
for "the gods of the heaven and the gods of the earth"
is an old Sumero-Accadian classification of the gods.

In order to insure completeness, one magician includes
this formula: "all the evil (—demons—) whose names are
mentioned in this bowl or whose names are not mentioned in this bowl."

So much for the demons and hostile forces that
make life so painful. Now the question is: How is one
to render the demons impotent? The symbol of render-
ing them harmless is that of tying, binding, or shackling
them. One of the formulae is "(All the evil spirits) are
bound, hobbled, and crushed under the left heel of (the
client)." Perhaps the praxis accompanying this incantation was the client's crushing of images under his left
heel. Another variant runs: "(All the spirits) are bound,
tied, and sealed. Their mouths are closed, their eyes are
blinded, their ears deafened, so that they cannot hear
anything against (the client)."

Once having bound and rendered them harmless, you
have then to use a formula of exorcism, to drive them
away from the body, the house, and the property of the
client seeking protection. One such formula reads: "Let
them get out of the 148 parts of his body; let them not
stand in his standing-place nor lie in his bed-chamber."
The fact that their being bound may impede their flight
does not bother the magician, and we constantly find

these contradictory combinations side by side in the same charm: "Upset, turned back and repulsed are all the curses and invocations of all women, men, boys, girls, evil foes and enemies that they have cursed and invoked by night and by day. They are bound and turned away from the four corners of my house."

There is a widespread belief that an undeserved curse will be, or may be, turned back upon the head of the curser. Thus cursing is only legitimate after an offense has been committed. We have these unmerited curses directed back to their source by such charms as this:

Bound are the hands and feet of the men and women who have worked evil against this Brikyabya son of Marat, and let all the evil spells be uprooted from this Brikyabya son of Marat and from his constellation and planet and from all his house and from all their dwelling, and let them be turned back and return and go to those that worked them and to those that sent them, from this day and forever, in the name of Yahweh, God of Hosts.

It is interesting to note that "from this day and forever" is a legal formula particularly common in bills of divorcement.

The situation is more complicated when the curse is deserved. Suppose you have injured someone, and out of the bitterness of his heart and not without justice, he has pronounced a malediction against you. You must then get him to consent to take back the curse and bless you so as to cancel it. There is a quaint Mandaean text in the Harvard Semitic Museum in which this procedure is reflected:

(The guardian angel) has seized them by the tuft of the hair of their heads and by the tresses of their pates and said to them: "Remove what you have cursed against this Abi daughter of Nanay." And they said to him: "From the anguish of our hearts we have cursed and from the bitterness of our palates we have resolved to curse." ... "I make you swear and I adjure you in the name of (the protecting angels) that you release and free Abi from all the curses and invocations that you have cursed; and from the curses of father and mother ... and from the curse of harlot and singing girl ... and from the curse of employee and employer who stole his wages from him, and from the curse of brothers who have not divided (the inheritance) fairly."

This is not quite reasonable, for not only are these supposed to take back the curses they themselves have uttered, but also the curses pronounced by other people under other circumstances. And then finally comes the adjuration to give the blessing that will cancel and neutralize the original curse: "(The curses are sent back) to those that pronounced them until they release, free and bless."

The specific ways of coping with demons are many and curious. First, you can adjure them and threaten them with dire consequences. There is one heroic figure named Qatros, whose lance kills demons and liliths; and if you threaten them with the lance of Qatros they become frightened and desist:

I adjure thee, Lilith Hablas, granddaughter of Lilith Zarnay, the lilith that lodges on the threshold of the house of this (client)...that smites, shakes, throws, strangles, and slays...boys and girls...I adjure thee that thou be smitten in the membrane of thy heart by the lance of the mighty Qatros.

Another way is to resort to divine authority either pagan or orthodox. In order to contend with a certain demoness who slays children, there is the following charm in the name of the old pagan gods:

O Murderess, daughter of the Murderess! Get out and depart from the presence of....The Sun has sent me against thee, the Moon has despatched me, Bel has commissioned me, Nanay has said to me...and Nergal has given me the power that I might go against the evil spirit, namely Dodib, whom they call the Strangler that kills babies in the bosom of their mother.—Get out from before these angels that sons may remain alive for their mothers and little children for their fathers.

And thus the killer is foiled. The magician may even appeal to the sixty male gods and eighty goddesses: the whole brood of pagan deities.

The Mandaeans have hypostatized Life, and their incantations often begin with the formula: "In the name of the great, strange, abundant, and lofty Life!" and end with the formula: "And Life is victorious!"

There may be an appeal to the Power "who puts to flight every spirit, male or female, that has changed his place and come to a place that is not his own from the days of creation."

Side by side with unorthodox invocations is the orthodox invocation in the name of God. Many of the incantations begin with the formula: "In Thy name do I act!"

One text is written in the name of the Lord but for a purpose that would hardly be looked upon with favor by the more conservative members of the community; for it smacks of black magic. But first we should refresh our memories regarding the difference between white and black magic. Black magic takes the initiative to hurt other people; white magic is to cancel or prevent harm to the client. Black magic is offensive; white magic, defensive. This text is one of the very rare examples of love philters. A woman named Ahat would obtain the love of a certain man by this spell: "In the name of the Lord of heaven and earth! This bowl is designed for the name of Anur—son of Parkoy, that he may burn and be kindled and inflamed after Ahat—in the name of the angel Rahmiel and in the name of Dlibat the passionate." Dlibat is one of the names of the goddess of love, and Rahmiel means literally "love angel"; so that not only the true God is invoked at the beginning, but also one of the Hebrew angels and a pagan goddess at the end. When I was working in the Museum of the University of Pennsylvania on some unpublished bowl texts I chanced on another love philter, and it was by the same woman, for the same man!

Sometimes the Great Name of God is appealed to and it is described as "the Great Name of which even the Angel of Death is afraid." There are many Old Testament quotations (nearly always in Hebrew; very rarely in Aramaic translation); and the orthodox guardian angels are often asked to give their protection.

Other sources of help are the seal of God and the seal of Solomon. Solomon has always enjoyed the reputation of a great master of spirits. Jewish literature, the Arabian Nights and numerous other sources commemorate his fame in this capacity. Both the seals of God and of Solomon are appealed to in this formula: "They, their house, their children and their possessions are sealed with the seal of El-Shadday, blessed be He, and with the seal of King Solomon son of David who worked spells on the male demons and female liliths."

We are not to expect any consistency or any unadulterated standard of orthodoxy in these texts. The community, as we have seen, was composite; and this is reflected in their angelology as well as in their demonology. Here pagan and Jewish elements are found side by side:

Bound and sealed are the house and garden of this Shabor son of Elisheba with seventy knots, seventy seals, seventy bonds, a chain, a rope, the seal of Yukabar-Ziwa son of Rabbe, the seal of the angel Kasdael, the great prince of the Chaldeans; the seal of the mighty angel

Gabriel, the prince of fire; the seal of the demon Aspa-
nadas, the jinnee of King Solomon son of David; and
with the seal of the Great Master of the universe, Whose
knot cannot be loosened and Whose seal cannot be
broken.

The orthodox at least may look with favor on the fact
that the climax is the seal of the Lord Himself, Whose
bond is supreme. God's bond is something that is to hold
the whole universe in check till the day of judgment.
One text reads thus: "I bind you with the bond where-
with the seven planets and twelve signs of the zodiac
are bound unto the great day of judgment and the great
hour of salvation."

There are various ways of dealing directly with
demons, as with people. One is the appeasement policy.
You may not like demons, but you can appease them by
offering them hospitality. Oriental hospitality consists of
welcoming the guest into your house, offering him food
and drink, and bringing him something to soothe his
skin, such as oil or perfume, or at least water to wash
his feet. One text gives, presumably in the name of the
client and not of the magician, the following formula:

I went up to the roof at night and said to them: "If
ye are hungry, come eat! And if ye are thirsty, come
drink! And if ye are dry, come be anointed! But if ye
are neither hungry, nor thirsty, nor dry, return and go
by the way on which ye have come and enter the house
from which ye went and enter the mouth from which
ye went."

In other words, the demons may be invisible to you, but you have done your best; you have invited them in, and offered them every possible hospitality. The fact that they have not accepted your hospitality, your meat, drink and oil, shows that they are perfectly satisfied, that they bear you no grudge, and that they will go back where they came from.

In one variant of this formula there is a definite refusal by the demons; presumably, since they evidently did not come in, the demons had declined the invitation: "We (the clients) went up to the roof and said: 'All ye bad spells, bad vows and hated practices that have passed by our door—enter!—here is meat to eat and here is wine to drink!' They opened their mouths and said to us: 'Who wants to enter your house?'"

The policy of intimidation is frequently attested in incantation literature. In the following there is intimidation by force of arms (as well as appeal to authority): "If ye say anything against (the clients), I am going to draw the bow against you and stretch the string against you. And if ye do anything (to the clients), I am going to bring down the decree of heaven and the ban which is upon Mount Hermon and the monster Leviathan."

One of the quaintest ways of dealing with demons is by the use of a certain legal procedure for divorce. In America divorce is a rather long-drawn-out and fairly costly process, which only the rich can usually afford and which even they cannot obtain quickly. But in the Orient a man can dismiss his wife without delay or difficulty. Accordingly, the divorce formulae were appropriated by the magician to drive out demons and particularly liliths:

Lo, I have written to thee! Lo, I have dismissed thee and lo, I have abandoned thee and lo, I have banished thee with a bill of divorcement!—Just as devils and demons write and serve (bills of divorcement) on their wives and they never return to them...so thou, O wicked lilith...take thy document of dismissal and thy letter of banishment and flee, fly, get out and depart from this (client and her husband)...and do not appear to them in visions of the day or in apparitions of the night, in the guise of either man or woman.

A great expert in serving bills of divorcement on liliths was Joshua son of Perahya, well-known in ancient Rabbinic literature, and whose authority is often cited in the bowls.

According to rabbinic law, if a wife and husband are living in different localities and the husband wishes to divorce the wife, he has only to send her a bill of divorcement, by mail or by messenger. As soon as she receives it in her hand, she is automatically divorced, even before it is read to her. That is the force of the phrase "take thy document." As soon as the lilith has touched it, she has to go.

In Chapter VIII we referred to the custom of expelling a disgraceful woman after stripping her of her clothing and driving her into the street naked (and with disheveled hair). These liliths are so described on being divorced: "Ye are stripped naked and not clad; your hair is disheveled." And there are pictures of liliths being divorced, showing them naked and with their locks of hair flying wildly.

Ancient magic beliefs still persist in our midst. The examples are too numerous and too familiar to warrant listing here. To cite only one widespread example, we may refer to the calling up of ghosts. The modern seance is of a piece with the episode of the witch of Endor, and can only be regarded as a disreputable heritage from remote antiquity.

Magic may perhaps not be altogether harmful. If a patient believes that a certain harmless pill is doing him good, I should not hold it against a doctor for giving the patient a placebo. But a doctor who would give his patient a placebo while failing to set a broken bone, would be definitely reprehensible.

What should alarm us most is not the survivals of ancient magic but what may be described as neo-magic; that is to say the contribution of our own generation to the long history of quackery. Pseudo-sciences that have no regard for causality are in many cases recognized and licensed by the laws of many of the states of this country. Thus quack colleges of pseudo-medicine are sanctioned in many parts of this land and the health of our citizens is entrusted in part to their graduates on footing similar in kind, if not in degree, with the legitimate medical profession. My former barber in Philadelphia, who had never got through grammar school, received his doctorate after a few months of night school study from a quack medical college chartered by the State of

Pennsylvania. He is now licensed to practice medicine on the theory that the various functions of the body are controlled by a series of "push buttons" on the spine. Such a theory which does not reckon with causality to any ascertainable degree, is essentially magical. This aspect of American life is as quaint as anything in the Aramaic bowls.

Human suffering brings about wishful thinking and makes the times riper for a widespread revival of magic. I may venture the prediction that the world is heading for a revival of magic because of the rapid spread of misery. When people lose their loved ones, for example, they are the more conditioned to turn to spiritualism so as to converse with those they love.

The quack always has the advantage over the scientist in that while the scientist can make limited promises, the quack can promise anything from cancer cures to Utopia. In desperate times, he who extends the greatest hope is the most welcome.

I do not go so far as to say that magic has no place in life. Possibly it is necessary for some people, as a kind of escape mechanism but I see little or no place for it in the lives of rational men and women. However, it is a great factor in life, even at present. The study of this subject, if not an antidote, may at least provide us with an understanding of a living problem.

CHAPTER XI

THE PAST STILL LIVES

AT THE moment they happen, events tend to assume a disproportionate prominence in the immediate vicinity, much as a stone thrown into water produces a local splash. It is the passage of time that sees a widening effect in both cases. Indeed some events become more and more important as time goes on. Thus the Phoenician invention of the alphabet becomes more significant as new nations adopt a form of it and as literacy increases.

Our noblest virtues (as well as our greatest failings) and our material civilization are rooted in the past. We have had occasion to note that our laws, ethics, morals, and religion stem in large measure from the Scriptures. Our superstitions no less than our sciences hark back in part to ancient Sumer and Accad. Our material civilization would be unthinkable without the metallurgy and mechanical devices that our ancient predecessors have bequeathed us. The wheel, the spring, the pulley and countless other fundamental inventions in remote antiquity have made our machine age possible.

The popular notion that the past is dead is simply untrue. The past still lives in us, whether we recognize it or not. We have not come by much of our culture through any ability or effort of our own. If we live in houses instead of caves, it is because of the material progress made in the East thousands of years ago. The working man enjoys a day of rest each week not because he has lifted himself by his bootstraps but because an old Hebrew institution still lives among us. Most of what we live is but a slightly modified inheritance from long ago. To be sure, the contributions of our own age are not to be slighted. Mechanical power and (what to me is far more significant) progress in medicine are great landmarks in culture. But even the greatest discoveries of our age are of less significance than the invention of writing in the fourth millennium B.C.

That the past lives in us will remain true, come what may. It is the study and awareness of the past that hang in the balance. We live in an age when men are divided more dangerously than ever before into hostile camps, as if there were no common ground on which all humanity could meet. This common ground is the respect for, and study of, the humanities. Culture and history unite not only the citizens of one land but nation with nation. The Americas and Europe have in common the traditions of Zion, Athens, and Rome. In repudiating these three basic sources of our culture (and our universities are among the offenders!) we are undermining one of the greatest hopes of the Occident. By putting a ridiculously high premium on "the present moment in our own back yard" we are destroying the basis for international harmony. I should even go a step farther than those who plead for the conventional classics: Since we live in a world with 400,000,000 people in China, with 350,000,000 in India, and with many other millions of non-Occidental origin, it is only a broad humanistic approach that can ever provide the world with an awareness of the universal humanity that unites all men.

If this little book has helped to widen the reader's concept of the human race, chronologically or geographically, it has fulfilled its purpose.

BIBLIOGRAPHICAL SUGGESTIONS

I HAVE purposely not burdened the reader with diacritical marks, footnotes, and text references. Perhaps I have gone too far, but in the interest of consistency I have left out even the chapter and verse numbers of Biblical quotations, just as I have not given text and line numbers of Ugaritic or Nuzian tablets. This may at times mystify some readers especially since my translations are from the original sources and my Scriptural citations need not tally with any of the printed English Bibles.

To compensate for the lack of technical apparatus on the preceding pages, I make the following suggestions for such readers as may wish to delve more deeply into any of the topics discussed in this book. These suggestions constitute only a key to the bibliography. The bibliography itself would be much bigger than this book.

For a broad treatment of the ancient Near East, see William Foxwell Albright's *From the Stone Age to Christianity*, The Johns Hopkins Press, 1940. The notes are a rich source for the bibliography.

Inasmuch as my field experience was obtained while I was engaged by the American Schools of Oriental Research, most of my archaeological material (Chapters I-V) is derived from expeditions of the Schools. The best way to begin a study of the work at the sites in question is to look through the files of the *Bulletin of the American Schools of Oriental Research,* where the preliminary reports have been published and final reports are referred to. Furthermore, the *Bulletin* is a sort of clearing house for studies of the ancient Near East in general, thanks particularly to the steady flow of comprehensive critical notices from the pen of the editor, Professor Albright.

The best work on the glyptic art of ancient Western Asia (Chapter VI) is H. Frankfort's *Cylinder Seals,* Macmillan Co., 1939. Much new source material has appeared in the two years that have elapsed since then. My publication of the collection in Walters Art Gallery (*Iraq* VI, 1939, pp. 4-34, pls. II-XV) came out shortly after Frankfort's book. For subsequent seal publications see the bibliography of the cuneiform world compiled periodically in the journal *Orientalia* by Professor A. Pohl, S.J., and myself under the title "Keilschriftbibliographie."

My *Ugaritic Grammar* (Pontificium Institutum Biblicum, 1940) may serve as a guide to the Ugaritic literature (Chapter VII). One may bring the bibliography up to date by glancing through the current issues of the "Keilschriftbibliographie."

The Nuzu source material (Chapter VIII) is referred to in my study of "The Dialect of the Nuzu Tablets" in *Orientalia,* 1938; see especially p. 32. Also in this field the literature may best be brought up to date through the "Keilschriftbibliographie." I have treated the status of woman in the Nuzu tablets in *Zeitschrift für Assyriologie* XLIII, 1936, pp. 146-169; and the Biblical parallels in

The Biblical Archaeologist III, pp. 1-12, Feb. 1940. As I now write (May 12, 1941), the published Nuzu tablets total about 1200 but Dr. E. R. Lacheman is about to bring out a volume of 380 new texts. It is in anticipation of Lacheman's volume that I have taken 1500 as the round number of the available Nuzu documents.

Professor Harry Torczyner published the Duweir texts (Chapter IX) first in an English edition: *The Lachish Letters,* Oxford University Press, 1938; and then in a Hebrew edition: *The Lachish Ostraca,* Jerusalem, 1940.

For the sources of Chapter X see the "Aramaic Incantation Bowls," which I have dedicated to my distinguished teacher, Professor James A. Montgomery, on the occasion of his seventy-fifth birthday, June 13, 1941; the study is appearing in three parts in *Orientalia* 1941.

INDEX

Abdu-r-Razzaq Lutfy Effendi, 117
Abi, 209
Abracadabra, 198
Abraham, 17, 176, 177
Accad(ian), 120, 121, 122, 123, 218
Achaemenian (Empire), 80, 98, 198, 203
Adad, 127
Adam, 201
Ader, 42, 44
Aeneid, 145
"afarit," 47
Africa, 15
Agnew, Ruth, 9
Ahasuerus, 203
Ahat, 211
Ahiyahu, 190
Ain Defiya, 32
Albright, William Foxwell, 9, 42, 44, 45, 46, 58, 90, 221, 222
Alexander (the Great), 52, 59, 80, 105, 202
Alexandrian, 198
Ali (Abu Ghosh), 25, 33
Allah, 23, 32, 33, 39, 41, 45, 48, 58, 79
Allenby Bridge, 25
Amarna, 187. See also Tell el Amarna.
Amarna Age, 133, 134, 156
American, 73, 97, 105, 117, 170, 198, 214, 217
American Schools of Oriental Research, 9, 156, 221; Bulletin of the, 222
Americas, The, 219

Amman, 25
Amminae, 165
Ammon, 22, 25, 42
Amorite(s), 129, 130
Amos, 136
Amurru, 130
Anat, 137, 139, 140, 141, 142, 143, 144, 145, 149, 151, 152, 154
Anathoth, 183
Anatolia, 73
Angel of Death, 212
Anglo-Saxon, 15, 188
Antiochus V, 53
Anur-, 211
Aqaba, 32, 33, 35; Gulf of, 27, 32, 34
Aqhat, 150, 151, 152, 153, 154, 155
Arab(s), 9, 22, 23, 25, 26, 27, 29, 30, 33, 40, 46, 53, 64, 75, 84, 87, 88, 89, 103, 104, 105, 106, 131, 134, 141, 173, 181, 202
Araba, 27, 28, 30, 31, 35, 39
Arabia, 50
Arabian Desert, 26, 35
Arabian Nights, 212
Arabic, 42, 44, 45, 47, 66, 75, 105, 198, 202
Aramaean, 201, 202
Aramaic, 16, 172, 198, 202, 204, 212, 217
"Aramaic Incantation Bowls," 223
Arili, 166
Arnon Gorge, 32
Arrap-ha, 156, 175
Arteya, 166
Ascalon, 134
Asherah, 137, 138, 140, 142, 143, 145, 148

Asia(tic), 15, 52, 59, 109, 134, 198.
See also Western Asia
Asia Minor, 129, 134
asinus onager, 57
Aspanadas, 213
Assur, 60, 131
Assyria, 51, 60, 64, 72, 76, 98, 116, 129
Assyrian, 60, 80, 129, 132; Late ——, 131; Middle ——, 80, 131; Old ——, 128, 129
Astarte, 86, 149
Athens, 219
Athtar the Terrible, 140
Auda, Sheikh, 26, 30, 33
Azeqa, 180, 183, 187, 191, 192

Baal, 125, 136, 137, 139, 140, 141, 142, 143, 144, 145, 146, 147, 150, 151, 153, 154, 186, 188
Babel, 115
Babylon, 182, 183, 193
Babylonia, 76, 81, 116, 119, 131, 196, 198, 199, 202, 203
Babylonian(s), 16, 133, 157, 182, 183, 184, 189, 191, 203
Bacchides, 53, 55
Bache, Charles, 108
Baghdad, 50, 79, 99, 100, 101, 105, 106, 116, 117
baksheesh, 47, 55, 77, 102, 110
Baruch, 186
Bashan, 22
Basra, 99
Bauer, Hans, 135
Bedouin(s), 26, 28, 40, 44, 83, 89, 173
Beer Sheba, 39
"beqa," 59
"Berlin to Baghdad Railway," 99
Beth ha Rafa(?), 190, 191
Beth Sur, 52, 53, 54, 58, 59
Bible, 17, 35, 36, 53, 66, 115, 128, 155, 179, 181, 182, 186, 188, 221. See also New Testament, Old Testament, Scripture(s), and Testaments

Biblical, 7, 17, 25, 123, 179, 180, 184, 221, 222
Biblical Archaeologist, The, 223
Botta, P. E., 60
Brikyabya, 208
British, 39, 60; pro-British, 90
British Museum, 116
Bronze Age, 74; Early ——, 42, 44, 56, 102; Middle ——, 42, 44
Bulletin of the American Schools of Oriental Research, 222
Burj es Sur, 54
Burrows, Millar, 9
Byzantine(s), 40, 54, 202

Cairo, 50, 133
Canaan, 73, 146, 187
Canaanite(s), 15, 17, 22, 124, 125, 135, 136
Cappadocian, 129
Carnarvon, 104
Carter, 104
Cassite(s), 130, 131, 157, 173
Catholic, 168
Central Powers, 135
Chaldeans, 212
Chicago, 152; University of, 67
China, 220
Christ, 37, 198
Christendom, 195
Christian(s), 15, 43, 44, 47, 82, 106, 202; Era, 115
Christianity, 194
Chronicles, 52, 168
"coat of many colors," 128
Colt Expedition, 40
Crusades, 22, 78
Cylinder Seals, 222
Cyrus, 194

Danataya, 150, 151
Daniel, 17, 136, 150, 151, 153, 154, 155
David, 16, 142, 182, 212, 213
Davis, Herbert, 9
Dead Sea, 27, 38, 62; Valley, 25
Devil-worshipers, 81, 82, 107

Dhorme, Edouard, 135
"Dialect of the Nuzu Tablets, The," 222
Divided Monarchy, 30
Dlibat, 211
Dodib, 210
Dominican Fathers, 36
"dragon-headed" symbol, 128
Duweir, 181, 223; *see also* Lachish *and* Tell ed Duweir

Ea, 122, 123, 124, 125
Early Dynastic (Age), 100, 120
Early Iron Age, *see* Iron Age
East, 171, 205, 219; *see also* Near East *and* Middle East
East Mediterranean, 133
Easter, 16
Eastern, 106
Eastern Roman Empire, 202
Easterners, 169
Ecclesiastes, 109
Edom, 22, 35, 36
Egypt, 18, 51, 52, 59, 73, 97, 102, 114, 132, 133, 134, 145, 179, 189, 190, 194, 198
Egyptian(s), 58, 61, 97, 133, 155, 182, 183; anti-Egyptian, 183
El, 136, 137, 138, 139, 140, 141, 142, 145, 147, 149, 150, 151, 152
el, 137
Eliezar, 176
Elisheba, 212
Elnatan, 190
El-Shadday, 212
Eluanza, 166
English, 16, 17, 90, 105, 139, 172, 185, 186, 187, 198, 205, 221
Englishman, 61, 99, 105
Enkidu, 123
Ennamati, 157
Eponyms, 57
Erbil, 105
Erech, 123
Esau, 177
esh shorba, 88
Esther, Book of, 203

Ethiopia, 198
Euphrates, 105, 124; Middle ——, 172
Europe(an), 73, 82, 100, 109, 198, 219
Eve, 201
Exile, 194
Exodus, 36, 37; Book of ——, 172
Ezekiel, 150, 155
Ezion Geber, 35

Fadhiliya, 76, 77
Farukdad, 201
Feast of Lights, 52
Fethi, 77, 78
First Dynasty (of Babylon), 128, 129, 130
France, 105, 149
Franco-Italian, 60
Frankfort, H., 222
Frankish, 78
Franks, 78
French, 105, 134, 135
Frenchman, 105, 135
From the Stone Age to Christianity, 221

Gabriel, 213
Gawra, *see* Tepe Gawra
Gaza, 103
Gemaryahu, 186
Genesis, 17
German(s), 135, 139, 172, 205
Gharandel, 32
Gilead, 22
Gilgamesh, 121, 123, 125; Epic, 121, 123
Ginsberg, H. Louis, 9
Glueck, Nelson, 9, 23, 29, 35
God, 23, 79, 81, 136, 137, 142, 176, 184, 188, 194, 195, 201, 212, 213; of Hosts, 208; *see also* Allah *and* Yahweh.
Great Zab (River), 98, 105
Grecian, 125
Greco-Syrian(s), 52, 53, 57, 59
Greece, 125

Greek(s), 16, 25, 39, 59, 125, 198, 202
Guweir, 99, 105

Habiru, 161, 162
Hablas, Lilith, 210
Hagab, 186
Hagar, 176, 177
Hajji, 90, 91
Halaf, 76, 114
Halhul, 53, 54
Hammurabi, 128, 129
Hamr Ifdan, 30, 31
Hana, 172
Haraya, 147, 148, 149
Hargab, 153
Harvard Semitic Museum, 209
Harvard University, 61
Hasan, 25, 32, 33
Head, R. G., 25
Hebrew(s), 16, 17, 22, 53, 59, 86, 125, 135, 136, 139, 172, 180, 181, 182, 185, 186, 187, 198, 211, 212, 219, 223
Hebron, 53, 54, 58
Hellenistic, 38, 55, 56; Age, 54; pre-Hellenistic, 114
Heracles, 125
Hermon, Mount, 214
Hilbishuh, 177, 178
Hinzuraya, 164
Hirihbi, 146
Hissilyahu, 186
Hittite(s), 73, 134
"Hocus pocus (dominocus)," 198
Hodoyahu, 189, 190
Homeric, 155; pre-Homeric, 121
Hosea, Book of, 172
Hoshayahu, 188, 189
Humerelli, 174
Hurrian(s), 73, 80, 129, 156, 157
Hydra, 125
Hyksos, 85

IGI-TA-NI, 128
Iliad, 145
Ili-Erish, 156, 157

India, 198, 220
Indo-European, 157
Inshallah, 32, 33
Iran, 202
Iraq, 100, 116, 117, 202
Iraq, 222
Iraq Museum, 99, 116, 117
Iraqian(s), 77, 99
Iron Age, 42, 74; Early Iron, II, 58
Isa, 89, 90
Isaac, 176
Ishmael, 177
Ishtar, 16
Islam, 34, 49, 194, 195, 198
Israel, 36, 128, 142, 180
Israelite, 56, 67, 85, 86, 97; anti-Israelite, 179
Israelites, 136, 176
Istanbul, 50
It-hiya, 156

Jaazaniah, 186
Jacob, 128, 162, 176, 177, 178
Jebel Bashiqa, 83
Jebel Ramm, 35, 36, 38
Jemdet Nasr (Age), 118, 119
Jeremiah, 66, 186, 188, 189, 192, 193, 194; Book of, 183, 189
Jericho, 64
Jerusalem, 23, 36, 39, 42, 52, 89, 180, 181, 182, 183, 184, 186, 190, 193, 223; pro-Jerusalemite 180
Jesus, 16, 182
Jewish, 52, 182, 202, 212
Jews, 16, 53, 194, 202
"jinn," 47
Job (Book of), 124, 155
Johns Hopkins Press, The, 221
Jonah, 148
Jordan, 25, 42; Rift, 22, 64
Jordan, Julius, 99
Joseph, 128
Josephus, 52
Joshua, 52; son of Perahya, 215
Judah, 52, 66, 84, 86, 180, 182, 183, 184, 188, 193

Judaism, 194
Judas (Maccabeus), 52, 53, 55
Judea, 72
Judean, 52, 66, 128, 180, 182, 188;
  pro-Judean, 179, 180
Judeans, 53, 57, 86, 189, 190

Kasdael, 212
Kathar-wa-Hasis, 137, 142, 143,
  145, 151
Kathirat, 146, 151
"Keilschriftbibliographie," 222
Kerak, 25
Keret, 147, 148, 149
Khalil, 54
Khawaja, 48, 49, 58, 90
khirba, 27, 53
Khirbet et Tubeiqa, 53, 54
Khirbet Nahas, 31
Khorsabad, 51, 60
Killi, 167
Kipteshup, 156
Kiripsheri, 171
Kirkuk, 99, 156
Kizaya, 166
Konyahu, 182, 183, 188, 190
Kurdish, 82, 83, 84
Kurds, 83, 84
Kurnub, 39
Kurpazah, 177, 178
Kushiharbe, 157, 173, 174, 175, 176
Kushuhari, 171

Laban, 178
Lacheman, E. R., 223
Lachish, 180, 183, 187, 191, 192,
  193
Lachish Letters, The, 223
Lachish Ostraca, The, 223
Late Assyrian, 131, 132
Latin, 59
Layard, Austen Henry, 60
Lebanon, 142
Leviathan, 125, 139, 214
"Lions," Tribe of the, 49, 50;
  Sheikh of the, 50

Lisan, The, 27
London, 101, 107, 133
Louvre, 116
Lullians, 161
Lulluland, 161
Lysias, 52, 53, 57

Maccabean(s), 52, 54, 56, 57, 58,
  59
Maccabees, First, 52, 57
Macmillan Company, The, 222
Mamshat, 58
Mandaean(s), 202, 208, 210
Mannuya, 166
Marat, 208
Mari, 105, 128
materia medica, 88
Mattanyahu, 183, 186
Matteshup, 178
Mattiya, 160
Mecca, 90, 91
Mediterranean, 133, 144
Megiddo, 31, 67, 68
Meneïya, 32
Meribaal, 185-6
Mesopotamia, 18, 73, 114, 115,
  124, 134, 179, 202; Southern,
  172
Mesopotamian(s), 116, 119, 122,
  134
Middle Assyrian, 80, 131
Middle East, 15
Milton, 17
Mishna, 191
Mitanni, 73, 165
Mivtahyahu, 186
Moab, 22, 35, 36, 43, 45, 46, 47,
  49, 50
Mohammed, 10; Sheikh, 45, 46,
  47, 49, 50
Montgomery, J. A., 223
Moon (god), 145, 146
Mormons, 16
"Mosaic," 176
Moslem(s), 44, 72, 79, 81, 82, 86,
  106, 168, 202
Mosque, 82

Mosul, 65, 72, 76, 79, 83, 99, 105, 106
Mot, 139, 140, 141, 143, 154
mufettish, 79, 107
Mycenean, 85

Nabatean(s), 32, 36, 37, 38, 42, 44, 45
Nanay, 209, 210
Near East, 8, 15, 17, 18, 21, 37, 60, 62, 65, 67, 73, 75, 94, 113, 126, 159, 161, 168, 169, 179, 204, 205, 221, 222
Nebuchadnezzar, 56, 66, 84, 86, 182, 183, 193, 194, 202
Neo-Babylonian, 115, 128, 182
Nergal, 210
Neriyahu, 186
"nesef," 59
New England, 16
New Moon, 151
New Testament, 182
New York, 107
Nikkal, 145, 146
Nile, 51, 52; Valley, 51
Nimrud, 60
Nineveh, 60, 79, 80
Niqmed, 138
Noah, 155
North Canaanite, 136
North Syria, 134
Northern Kingdom (of Israel), 128, 179
Nuzu, 129, 156, 157, 158, 161, 162, 165, 167, 169, 170, 171, 172, 173, 176, 177, 178, 222, 223
Nuzian(s), 158, 172, 221

Obeid, 76, 114
Occident, 15, 16, 108, 219
Occidental, 66, 187; non-Occidental, 220
Old Assyrian, 128, 129
Old Testament, 136, 137, 139, 141, 168, 176, 179, 180, 186, 212
Orient, 70, 214
Oriental, 72, 103, 107, 109, 205

Oriental Institute, 67
Orientalia, 222, 223
Oxford University Press, 223

Pagan Aramaic, 202
Paghat, 153, 154
Palestine, 16, 22, 28, 32, 40, 41, 103, 114, 134, 179, 181, 182, 187, 193
Palestinian 32, 56, 180
Paradise, 79
Paris, 107
Parkoy, 211
Parrot, André, 105
Patriarchal Age, 176, 177
Pebel, 147, 148, 149
Pennsylvania, Museum of the University of, 211; State of, 216-217
Perahya, 215
Persia(n), 80, 98, 194, 202
Peshkillishu, 174, 175
Petra, 32, 38
Petrie, Sir Flinders, 61, 102, 103
Pharaoh(s), 133, 134
Philadelphia, 25, 101, 216
Phoenician, 16, 135
Pohl, A., 222
Poltergeist, 205
Pontificium Institutum Biblicum, 222
Porada, Edith, 9
Promised Land, 36
Protestant, 168
Psalmist, 10
Psalms, 137
Ptolemies, 59
Pueblos, 62
Puhishenni, 156, 166
Purves, Pierre, 9
"pym," 59

Qadesh-Amrar, 142, 145
Qamoy, 201
Qart Abilim, 152, 154
Qatros, 209, 210
Qir-Moab, 25

Qoran, 82

R. A. F., 84
Rabbe, 212
Rabbinic(al), 202, 215
Rachel, 178
Rahmiel, 211
Ramadan, 81, 82, 84
Red Sea, 35
Rehoboam, 52
Reisner, George A., 61
Rhodes (Island of), 57
Rhodian, 57
Rockefeller, John D., 160
Roman(s), 16, 32, 37, 85, 202
Rome, 219

Sabbath, 16
Sabbatical Year, 53
Sahib, 77, 78
St.-John-the-Baptist Christians, 202
salugi, 75-6
Sapan, 137, 140, 144, 145
Sarah, 176
Sargon of Accad, 120; of Assyria, 51
Sasanian, 199, 203
Satan(ic), 81, 82, 124
Saty Beg, 117
Saul, 185
Saushattar, 165
Sbeita, 40
Schliemann, Heinrich, 61, 66
Scriptural, 221
Scripture(s), 16, 59, 86, 172, 176, 179, 181, 182, 187, 189, 218; *see also* Bible
Seleucid(s), 52, 57, 202
Seleucus, 52
Sellers, Ovid, 9, 55
Semakyahu, 190, 191
Semel, 154
Semite, 41, 120
Semitic, 16, 120, 121, 157
Sennacherib, 86
Shabor, 212

Shahar, 138
Shakespeare, 17
Shalem, 138
Shallum, 189, 190
Sheba, Queen of, 35
Shemayahu, 191
Shibaniba, 80
Shilwateshup, 158, 169
Shitanka, 165, 166, 168
Shurihil, 171
Shuwarhepa, 169
Shylock, 17
Sidonians, 148
Simon, 53, 55
Sinai, 40, 41
Smith College, 9
Solomon(ic), 30, 31, 32, 35, 67, 212, 213
Solomon's mines, 31, 32
Song of Songs, 141
South Arabian, 35
Southern Kingdom, 179
Starkey, J. L., 180
Strangler, 210
Sumer, 218
Sumerian(s), 16, 98, 100, 104, 119, 120, 127
Sumero-Accadian, 115, 207
Sumero-Babylonian, 196
Susan, 16
Susanna, History of, 17, 150
Sun (god), 125, 129, 210
Syria, 134
Syriac, 202
Syrian, 134; Desert, 128

"Tablets of Destiny," 124
Tacitus, 172
Takku, 157
Tehiptilla, 156, 158, 160, 161, 163, 164, 165, 170, 173
Tell Beit Mirsim, 72, 84, 87, 88, 89, 90, 97
Tell Billa, 72, 79, 80, 81, 82, 98, 104, 107
Tell ed Duweir, 180, 193; *see also* Duweir

Tell el Ajjul, 103
Tell el Amarna, 51, 133, 134; *see also* Amarna.
Tell en Nasba, 186
Tell Kheleifa, 35
Temple, 52, 194
Ten Commandments, 15
Tepe Gawra, 65, 72, 73, 75, 76, 80, 81, 95, 97, 98, 104 107, 108, 109, 111
Testaments, 16
Third Dynasty (of Ur), 100, 127, 128, 129
Third Early Dynastic, 120
Tigris, 124
Torczyner, Harry, 223
Toviyahu, 189, 190
Tovshillem, 186
Tower of Babel, 115
Transjordan(ian), 22, 37, 38
Tree of Knowledge, 124
Troy, 61, 147
Tulpunnaya, 158, 165, 166, 167, 168
Tupkitilla, 177, 178
Turkish, 111
Turks, 90, 91
Turshenni, 156
Tutankhamen, 104
Two Deeps, The, 124, 137
Tyrians, 148

Udm, 147, 148
Ugarit(ic), 10, 17, 125, 134, 135, 136, 137, 138, 139, 140, 144, 155, 221, 222
Ugaritic Grammar, 10, 222
United States, 197
Ur, 73, 98, 100, 103, 107, 111, 116, 120, 127
Ur III, 100
Uruk, 80, 114, 115, 118, 122, 123, 198
Utopia, 217

Valley of the Kings, 97
Venus, 16

Virolleaud, Charles, 135, 149
Vulcan, 137, 142

Wady Yitm, 35
Walters Art Gallery, 222
"wavy-ledge" handles, 102
West, 169
Western, 16, 106, 195
Western Asia(tic), 18, 51, 114, 117, 126, 128, 132, 133, 183, 222
Western Palestine, 22
Woolley, Sir Leonard, 98, 100, 101, 102, 103, 104
World War, 39, 91, 135

Xerxes, 203

Yaäzanyahu, 186
-yahu, 185
Yahweh, 15, 86, 125, 136, 137, 139, 141, 142, 185, 186, 187, 188, 189, 190, 191, 192, 194, 195, 208; *see also* God
Yahwism, 22, 183
Yamm, 143
Yarih, 145
Yatpan, 152, 154
Yaüsh, 187, 188, 189, 190, 192, 195
Yehoyakin, 182
Yezidi(s), 81, 82
Yirmiyahu, 186
Yukabar-Ziwa, 212
Yusuf, Mukhtar, 58; Sheikh, 49, 50

Zabinta, 201
Zarnay, Lilith, 210
Zarq, 201
Zedekiah, 182, 183, 186, 189, 192, 193
zeit el khirwa, 88
Zeitschrift für Assyriologie, 222
ziggurat, 51, 115
Zigi, 169, 170
Ziliptilla, 175
Zion, 194, 219
Ziph, 58
Zu-bird, 123, 124